Lives of

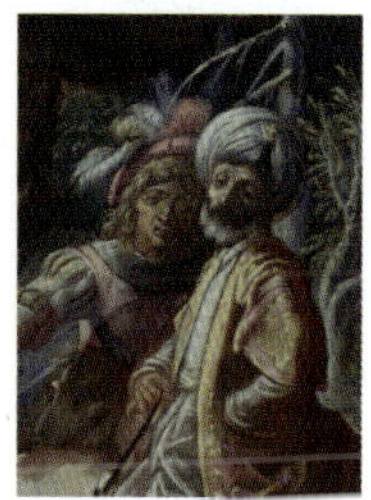

Elsheimer

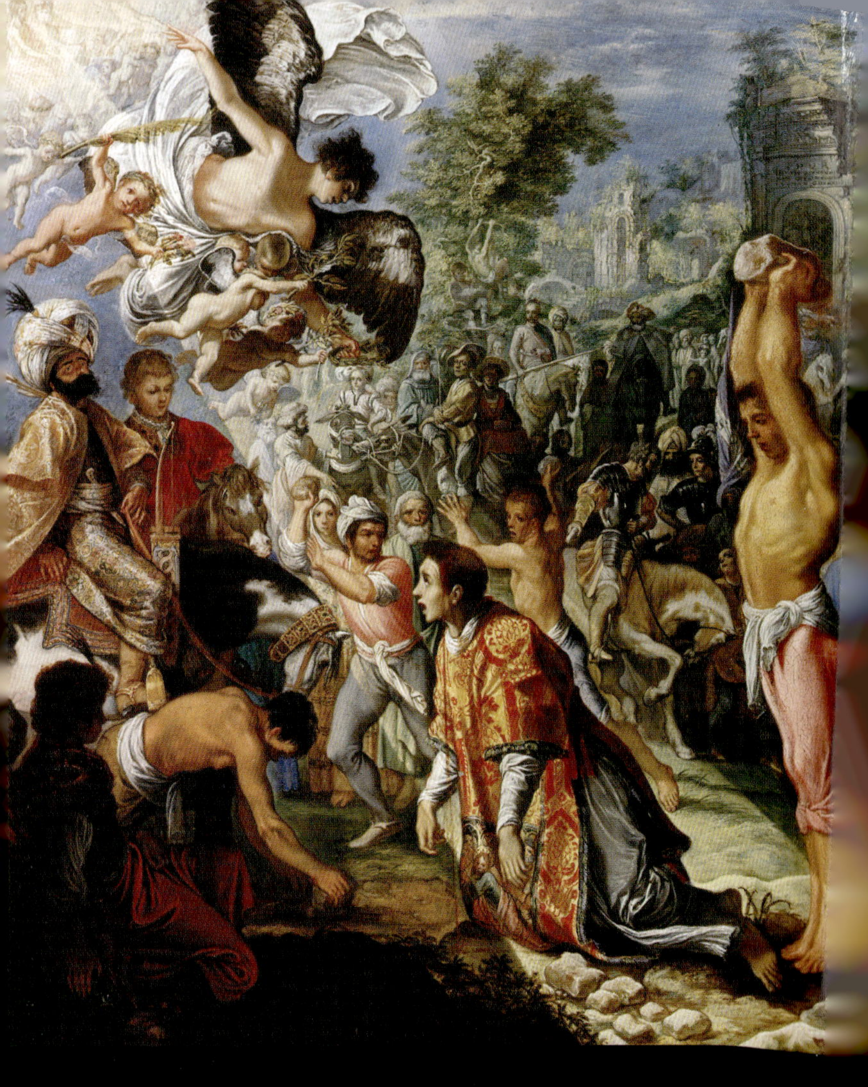

LIVES OF

ELSHEIMER

BY

CAREL VAN MANDER
GIULIO MANCINI
JUSEPE MARTINEZ
JOHANN FABER
GIOVANNI BAGLIONE
JOACHIM VON SANDRART
AND
JEAN-BAPTISTE LE BRUN

with an introduction by
CLAIRE PACE

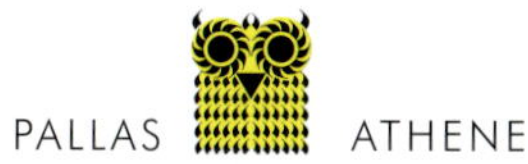
PALLAS ATHENE

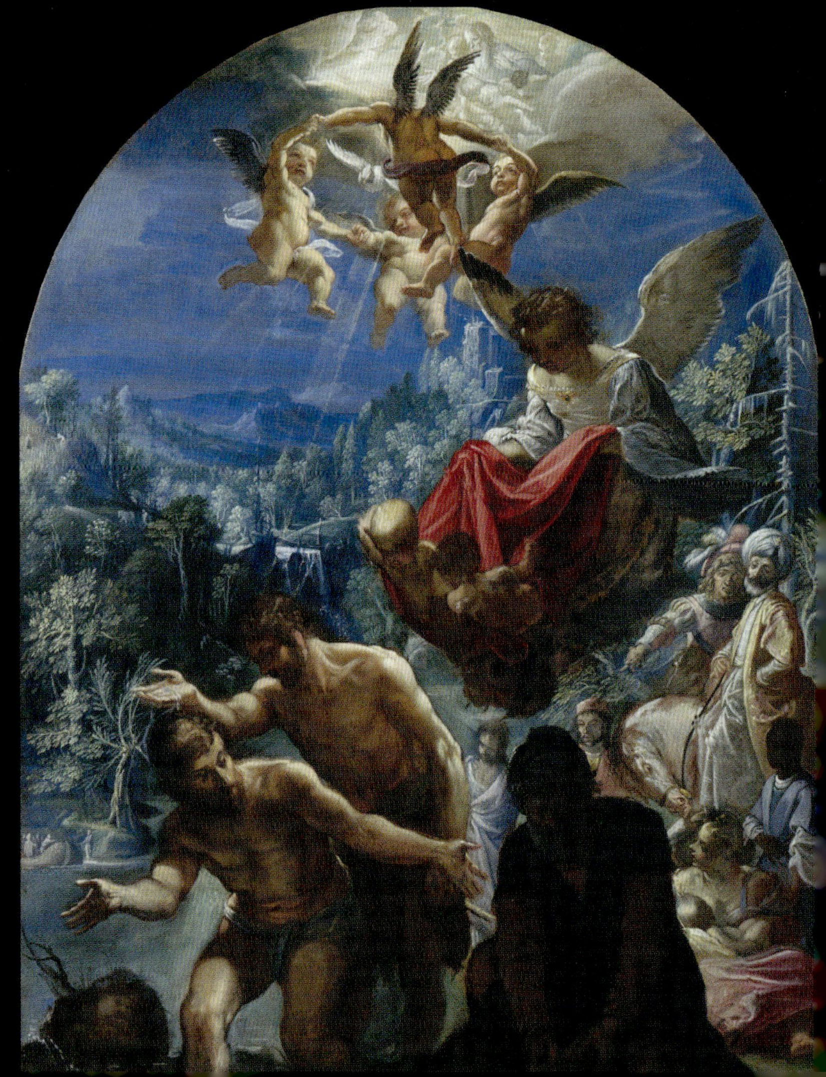

CONTENTS

Introduction by

CLAIRE PACE
p. 7

Lives of Elsheimer

CAREL VAN MANDER
p. 37

GIULIO MANCINI
p. 41

JUSEPE MARTINEZ
p. 45

JOHANN FABER
p. 51

GIOVANNI BAGLIONE
p. 55

JOACHIM VON SANDRART
p. 63

JEAN-BAPTISTE LE BRUN
p. 85

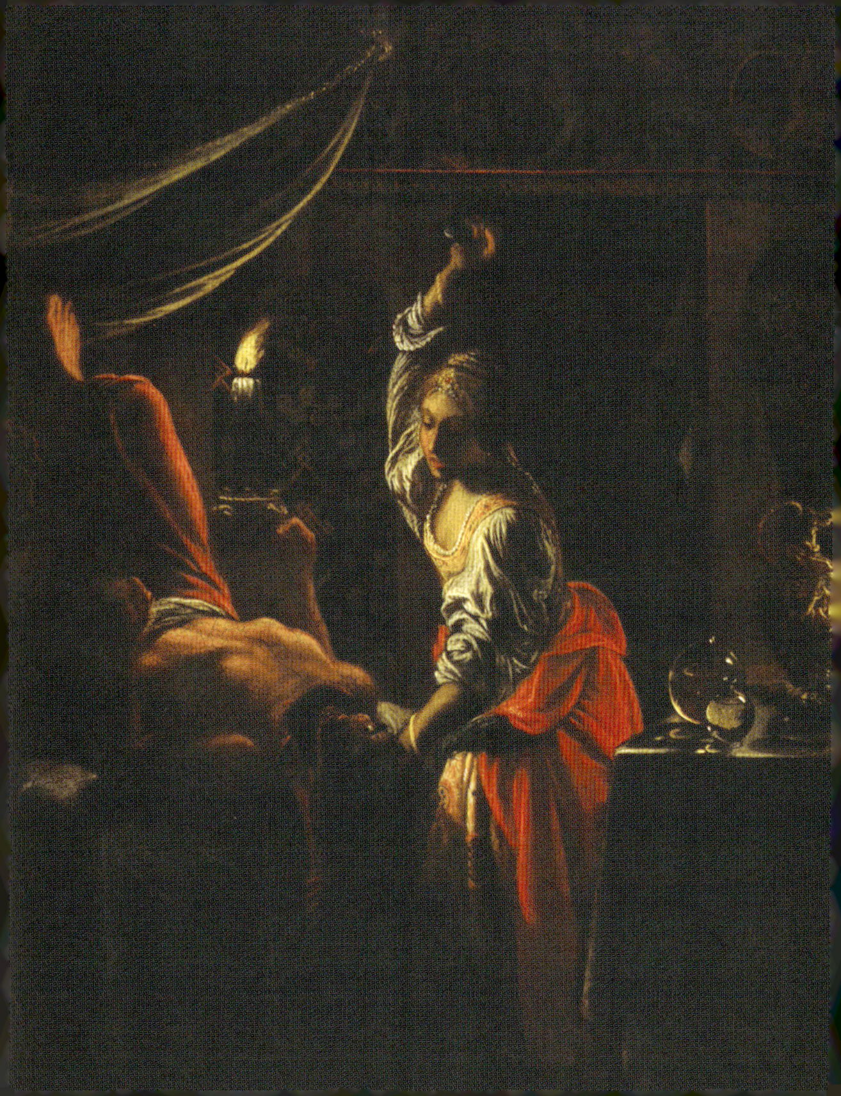

INTRODUCTION

CLAIRE PACE

On hearing of the death of Elsheimer, at the age of 32, Rubens wrote to Johannes Faber: 'Surely, after such a loss, our entire profession ought to clothe itself in mourning. It will not easily succeed in replacing him; in my opinion he had no equal in small figures, in landscapes, and in many other subjects.'

This gives an indication of the impact that Elsheimer's work had in his lifetime – an impact quite out of proportion to his short life, restricted output, and indeed the physical scale of his works. He was celebrated for his virtuosic skill in painting highly detailed compositions, on a miniature scale, on copper; in 1648 the miniaturist Edward Norgate asserted that the Italians described Elsheimer as il diavolo per glie cose piccole *('devilishly good at small things'). The copper surface gives a smooth and luminous quality to his work, which is characterised by a delicate refinement of handling. We associate him*

Opposite: Judith and Holofernes, c. 1601–3. This painting once belonged to Rubens

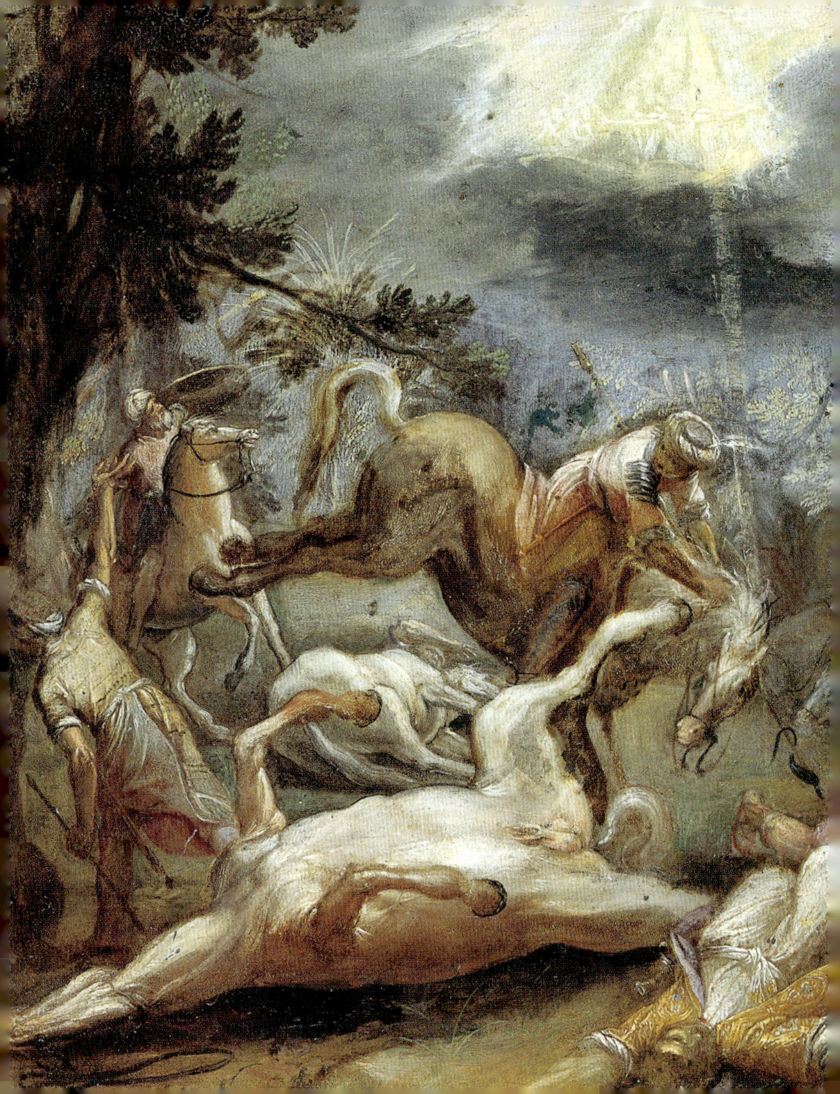

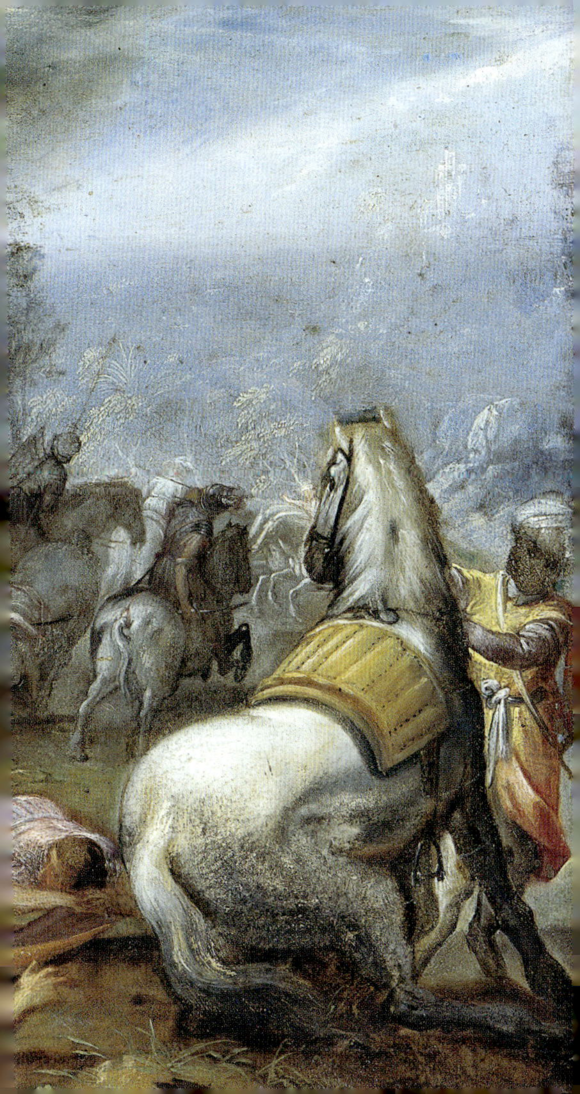

particularly with the creation of an idyllic and poetic landscape, often with artificial and nocturnal light effects – an evocation of landscape that would influence the muralist Agostino Tassi and Claude, as well as Dutch Italianate artists in Rome. Elsheimer was, however, equally known for his narrative and dramatic skill in multi-figural compositions of biblical or Ovidian subjects, and for this he was admired by Rubens and Rembrandt, who copied or adapted figures from his paintings. His œuvre is remarkably wide-ranging, from panels of single standing saints, to complex multi-figural compositions, and including interior scenes as well as those in which landscape plays a significant role.

Documentation about Elsheimer's life is scarce: for much of our knowledge we rely on the early biographies, especially that of Sandrart. He was baptised in Frankfurt in 1578, the eldest son of a tailor, and was probably a pupil of Philip Uffenborch, a leading local artist, whose grounding in artistic theory is emphasized by Sandrart. His training and early influences were very much in the German tradition of Dürer and Altodorfer (and his

Previous pages: The Conversion of St. Paul, c. 1598-9. Thoroughly German in its sources, this may have been painted in Bavaria on the way to Venice

earliest known painting, A Witch, *is a copy of a Dürer engraving); recollections of this tradition persist in his later work. It may be significant that he worked with stained-glass painters, and designed an armorial window – the jewelled colouring of his paintings recalls that of stained glass. In 1598 or 1599 he travelled to Venice, where he was associated with the Munich painter Rottenhammer, and clearly studied the works of Venetian artists, especially Veronese and Tintoretto. By April 1600 he was in Rome, and remained there until his death in 1610. In Rome he was part of a humanist circle surround ing Johannes Faber, the papal herbalist – a circle to which Rubens also belonged. Faber's warm personal tribute to Elsheimer – 'a regular guest in my house' – is printed here. He singles out particularly the* Mocking of Ceres, *(Bader Collection, Milwaukee), again a night-piece, but also praises the artist's ability to capture 'the true essence of nature', especially in 'paesi'.*

In 1606 Elsheimer married, and became a member of the artists' academy, the Accademia di S. Luca. At about the same time, he converted to Roman Catholicism. He

Overleaf: The Flood, c. 1599. This painting was probably painted in Venice and shows the strong influence of Rottenhammer and Jacopo Bassano

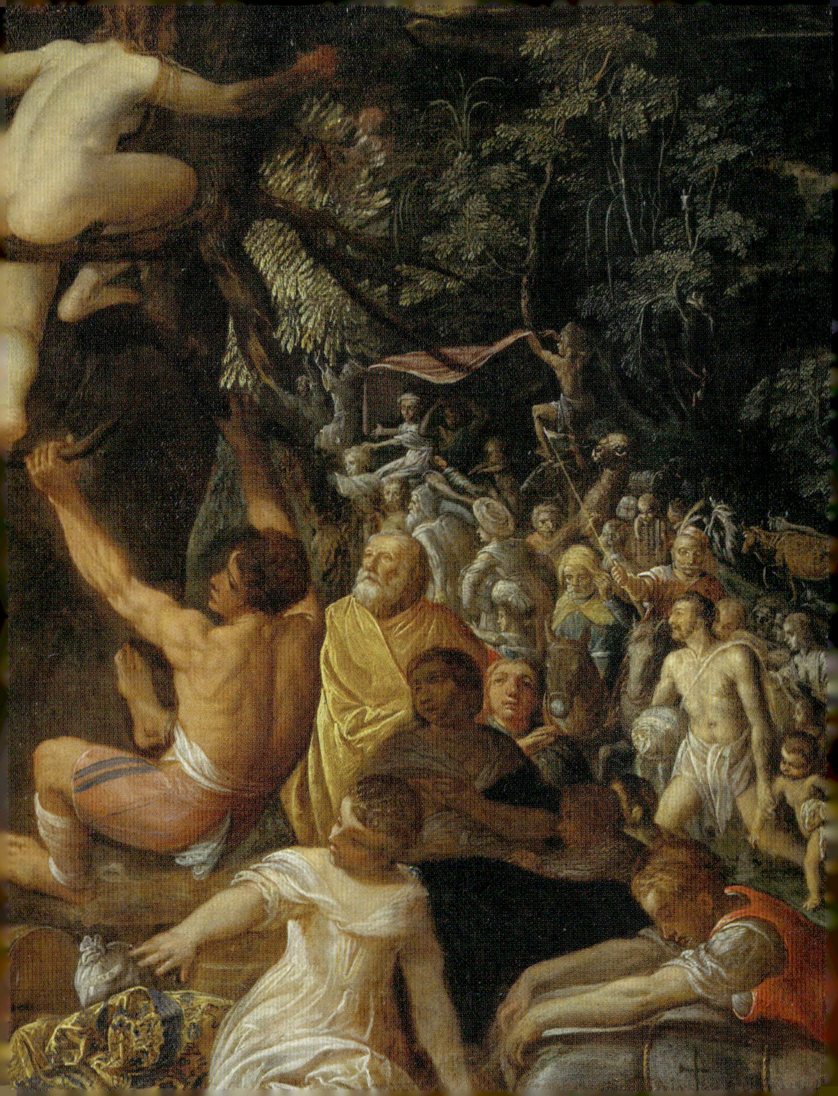

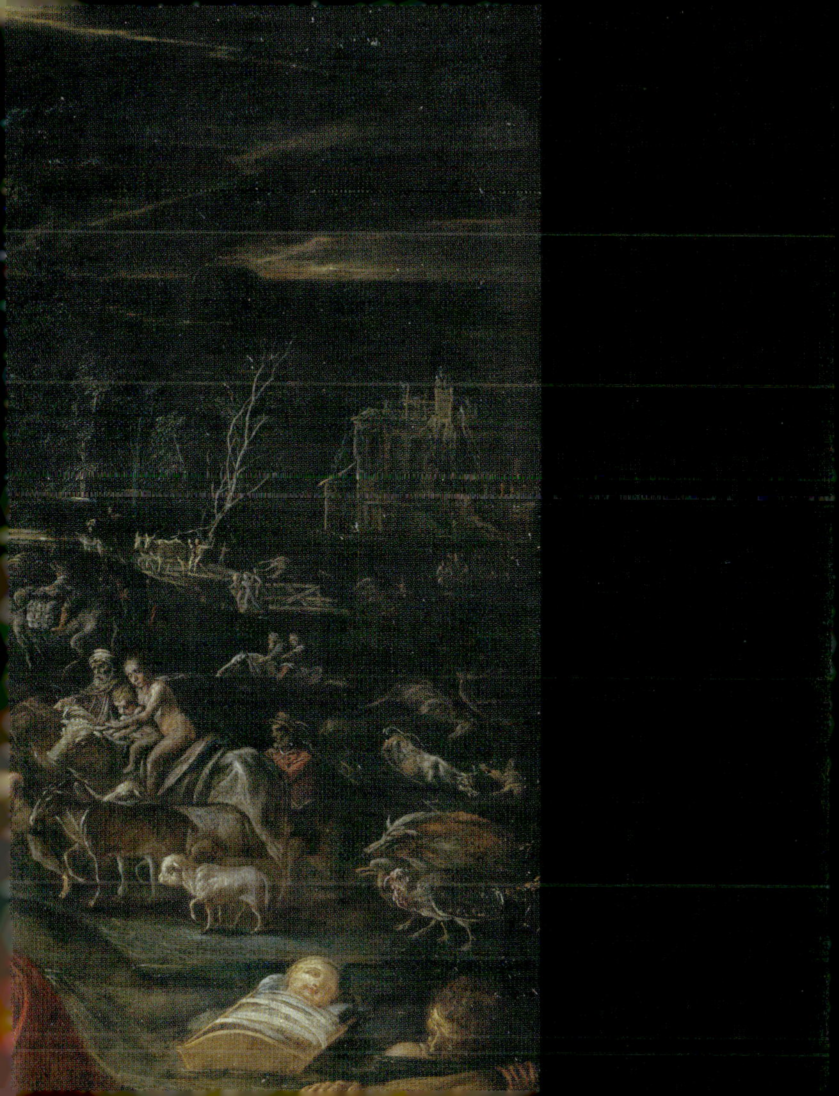

appears to have had a remarkably retentive visual memory – Van Mander (writing in 1604) says that he 'did not busy himself with drawings'. His work has affinities with that of some of his great Roman contemporaries, such as Caravaggio (he may have collaborated with Paul Bril), and echoes too of Venetian art and his German heritage (especially Altdorfer), while remaining entirely personal and individual.

Thus his dramatic use of various light effects may derive as much from Altdorfer or Bassano as from Caravaggio's contemporary experiments – though his uncharacteristically rhetorical use of gesture in the Three Maries *(Bonn, Landesmuseum) recalls both Caravaggio and Annibale Carracci, and his* Judith and Holofernes *(London, Wellington Museum) is surely indebted to Caravaggio's version. While his landscapes often recall Altdorfer or Venetian precedents, there are specifically Roman references in them also; we may conclude that he is both a German* and *a Roman artist, and it was in Rome that his art reached maturity and fruition.*

By temperament, Elsheimer appears to have been

Opposite: The Three Maries at the Grave, c. 1603. This painting once belonged to Paul Bril

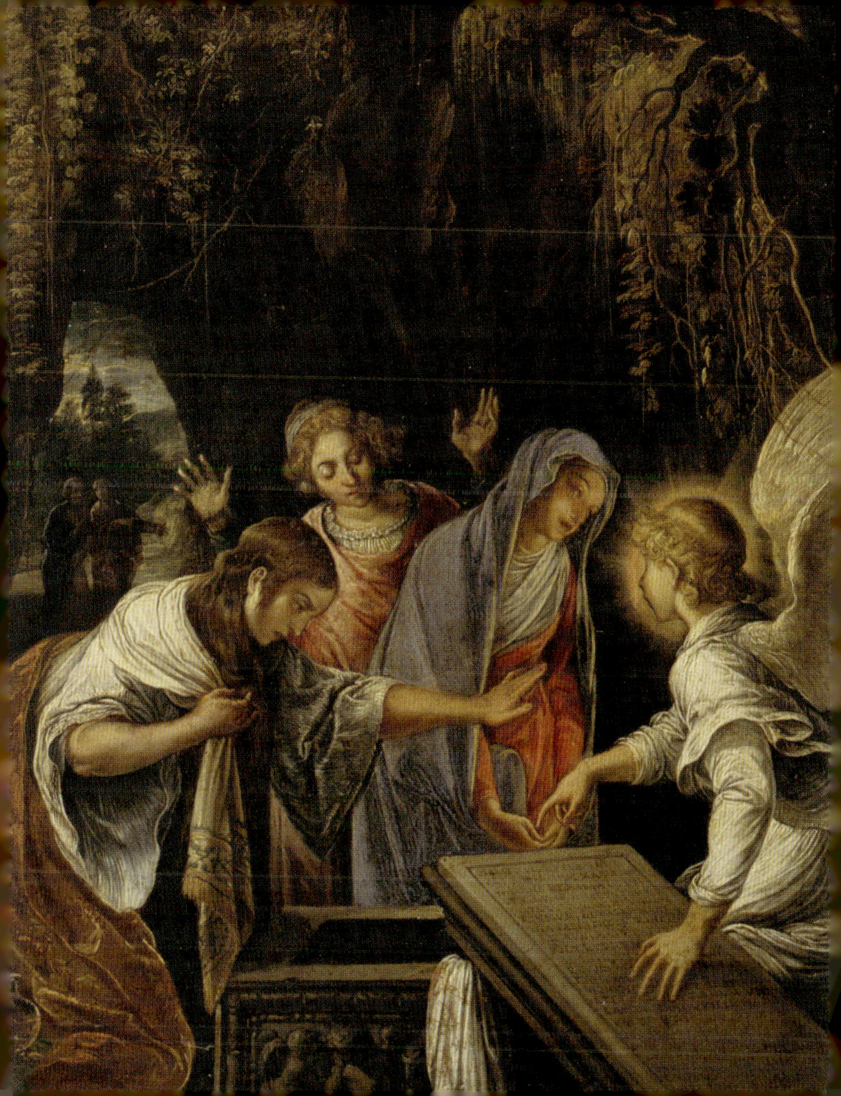

withdrawn and melancholic, as Sandrart describes him, qualities also suggested by his self-portrait, the only work on canvas (Florence, Uffizi). His method of working was slow and methodical; his lack of productiveness was attributed by the supremely energetic Rubens to accidia *(sloth). A number of his paintings are unfinished (as Baglione notes), and some have been overpainted. He worked with a fine brush – and possibly with the use of a magnifying glass – to render the meticulous detail. None of his works is signed, and of the Roman works only the* Flight into Egypt *(Munich, Alte Pinakothek) is dated (1609), so that establishing a definite chronology is difficult and partly conjectural. Some dates appear on the remarkable engravings after his work by the Dutch engraver Hendrik Goudt, who lived in his household, and appears to have been both pupil and patron, owning some of his works. According to Sandrart's account, the cantankerous Goudt quarrelled with Elsheimer, and forced him into the debtors' prison for failing to supply enough paintings, though there is no documentation for this assertion. It is undeniable, however, that Elsheimer did end his life in considerable poverty, as indicated by the inventory drawn up for his widow after his death.*

Ironically, despite this poverty, his paintings commanded high prices; Rubens wrote from Antwerp to Faber after Elsheimer's death that he would dearly like the Flight into Egypt *to be sent to Flanders, but feared that the price of 300 crowns asked by the painter's widow would be too great. We have little information about any commissions Elsheimer might have received, but there seems to have been a ready market at the time among noble Roman families for small-scale highly finished cabinet pictures, as evinced in inventories of their collections. In particular, Cardinal del Monte (Caravaggio's early patron) is recorded as owning* due paesini *by Elsheimer, and Scipione Borghese favoured northern painting, while* Il Contento *(Edinburgh, National Gallery of Scotland) may have been owned by Odoardo Farnese. Mancini describes how the 'princes' who owned his paintings guarded them secretively; Baglione comments on how rarely his works were seen, observing that their small size meant that they would be overshadowed in public exhibition. Elsheimer's paintings were highly prized in other European countries also; several were in English collections in the seventeenth century –* The Witch *(Hampton Court, Royal Collection) is listed in Charles I's 1639 inventory, and the Earl of Arundel and the Duke of Buckingham were also early admirers of his work. These*

Overleaf: The Realm of Venus, c. 1607-8. One of a set of three paintings that belonged to the Earl of Arundel

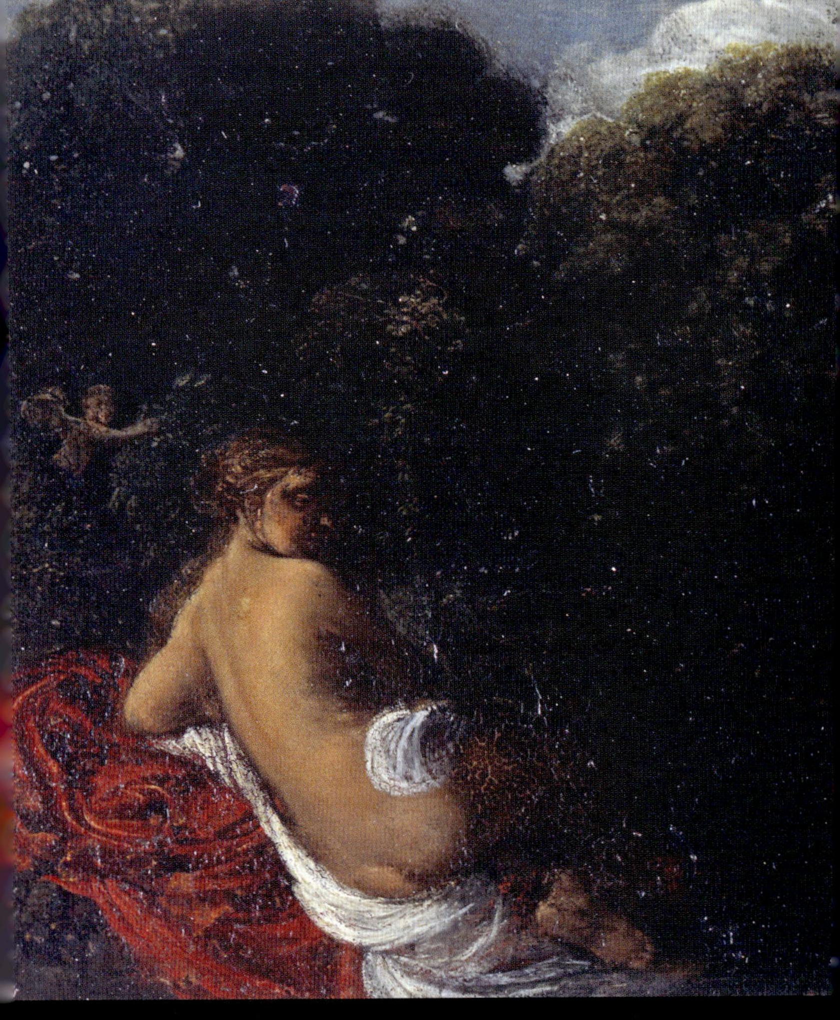

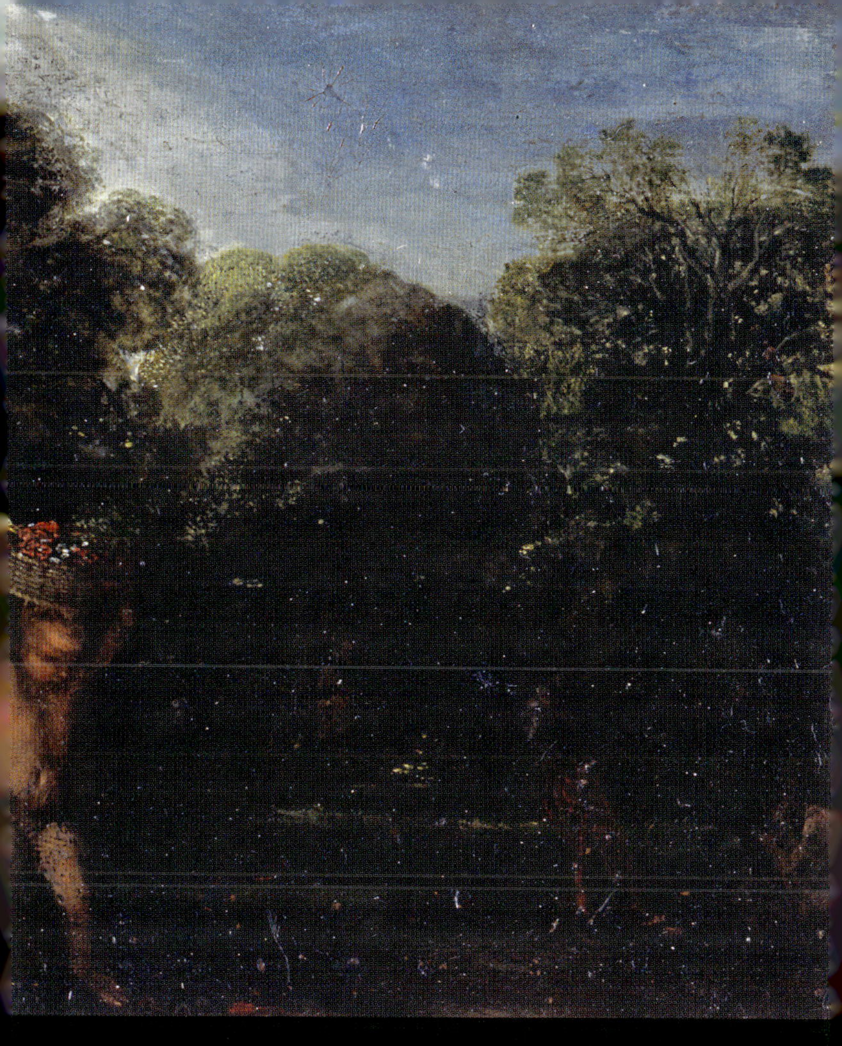

jewelled, highly wrought paintings chimed with the contemporary passion for 'curiosities'.

Elsheimer's international reputation is mirrored in the fact that of the six contemporary accounts printed here, two are Italian, and the others are French, Dutch, Spanish, and (the longest) German. The earliest biography printed here is by Carel van Mander (1548-1606), born in Flanders, a writer as well as an artist. He was apprenticed in Ghent, and in 1573 travelled to Italy. By 1584 he was a member of the Haarlem Guild of St Luke (as a Mennonite, he took refuge in the northern Netherlands). His short Life of Elsheimer *– the only one published in the artist's lifetime and the first mention of his name in a publication – appeared in his* Schilder-boek *(1604), in a section devoted to 'famous Netherlandish and High German painters'. Van Mander emphasizes Elsheimer's technical virtuosity, at least during his Roman period, and his remarkably retentive visual memory; he describes his habit of studying works of art intensively, dispensing with drawings.*

The next biography is by Giulio Mancini (1558-1630), physician to Urban VIII; it is from a treatise, Considerazioni sulla pittura, *written around 1614-21, which circulated in manuscript (not published until 1956).*

Mancini's treatise was widely known (a copy was owned by Cassiano dal Pozzo, Poussin's early patron), and is important both for information concerning provenance and as exemplifying early seventeenth-century taste. His approach stresses æsthetic judgement, anticipating that of the connoisseur; he writes that his aim is 'to consider the various means by which a dilettante (un huomo di diletto) *of similar learning as myself can easily pass judgement on paintings, collect them and display them.' His short piece on Elsheimer expresses this emphasis on an æsthetic response, praising the artist's 'marvellous' skill in 'design, finish, colour and grace'. It is interesting that he singles out the 'night-pieces' for special mention – Elsheimer's paintings in this vein – for example the* Mocking of Ceres, Philemon and Baucis *(Dresden, Staatliche Kunst-sammlungen), and of course the* Flight into Egypt *– accorded with a Europe-wide taste for such scenes in the early seventeenth century. Mancini mentions the quarrel with Goudt, though claims that the two were later reconciled, and his description of the 'great honours' accorded to the artist on his death, and the 'great sorrow' felt by fellow artists, who attended his funeral, attests again to the high esteem in which Elsheimer was held by contemporaries.*

Overleaf: The Realm of Minerva, c. 1607-8. Second of the set of three paintings that belonged to the Earl of Arundel; the third is lost

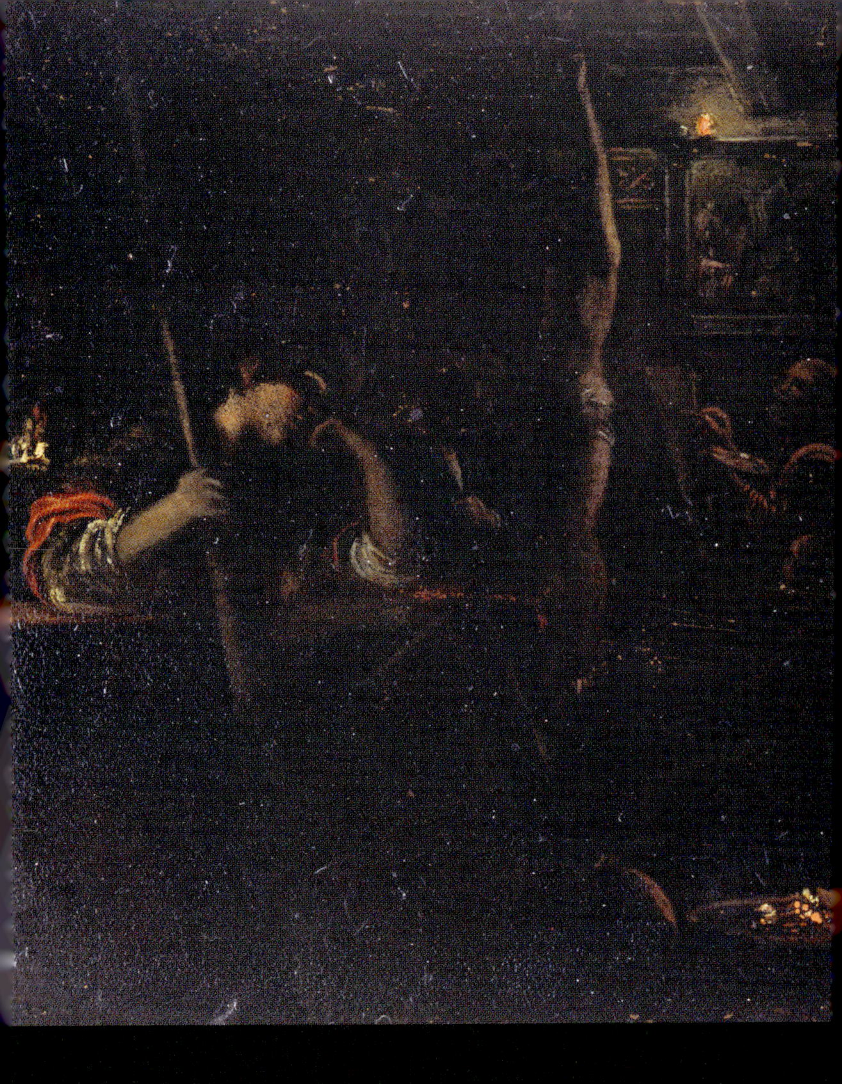

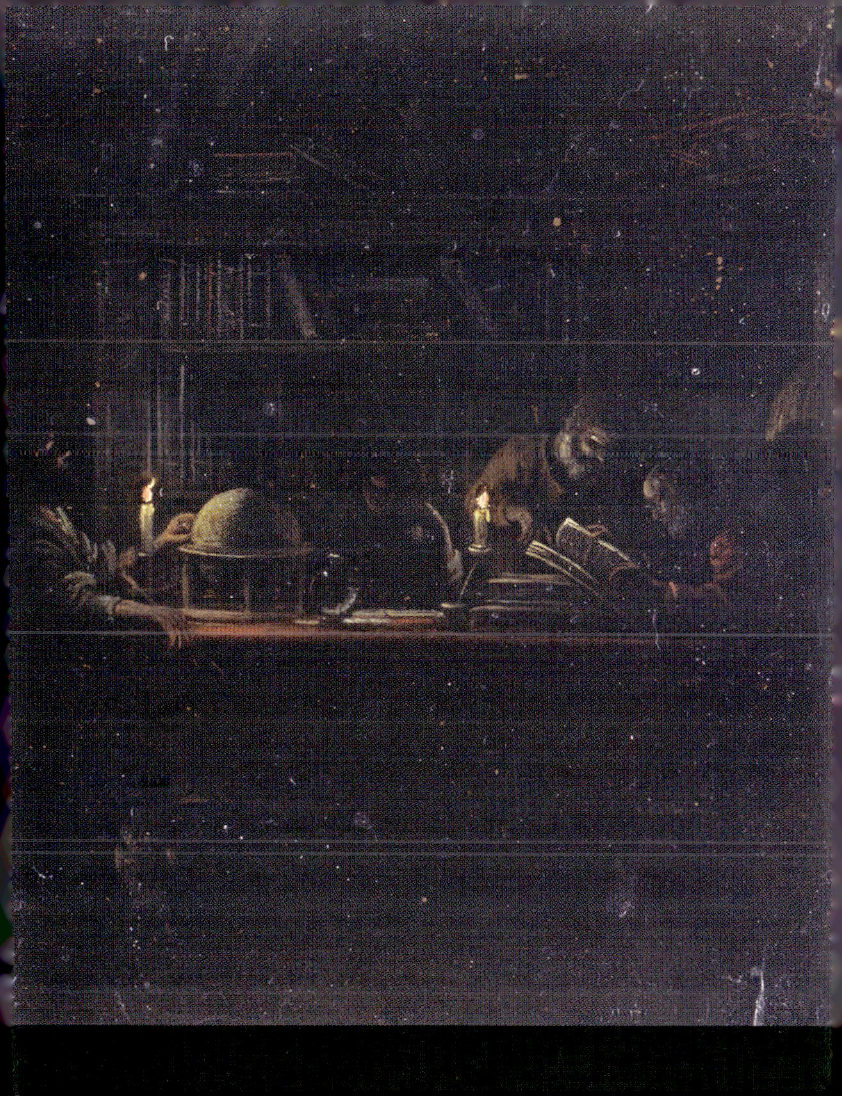

Another witness to this continuing reputation is the short memoir by the Spanish painter Jusepe Martinez, who was in Rome in 1625, when he was taken to see the painting now called The Exaltation of the Cross, *part of the Frankfurt Tabernacle. His admiring account appeared in his* Discorsos practicabile *(written c. 1673 but not published until 1866), and is also notable for the' detailed description of Elsheimer's melancholic and introspective temperament (corroborated by other biographers).*

The second biography is also by an Italian – indeed chauvinistically Roman – writer, Giovanni Baglione (c. 1573-1644) , who – unlike Mancini - was also a practising artist, perhaps best known for his vituperative quarrel with Caravaggio. His volume of more than 200 biographies of artists who had worked in Rome since 1572, published in 1642, was arranged in chronological order according to date of death, and grouped by pontificates up to that date (Elsheimer falls within the pontificate of Paul V). All the artists about whom he writes were dead, with the sole exception of Baglione himself; in his autobiography he states that he 'upheld the decorum of his profession, defended and honoured his profession and earned

Opposite: St Paul, c. 1605. Part of a group of paintings of saints: see p. 39

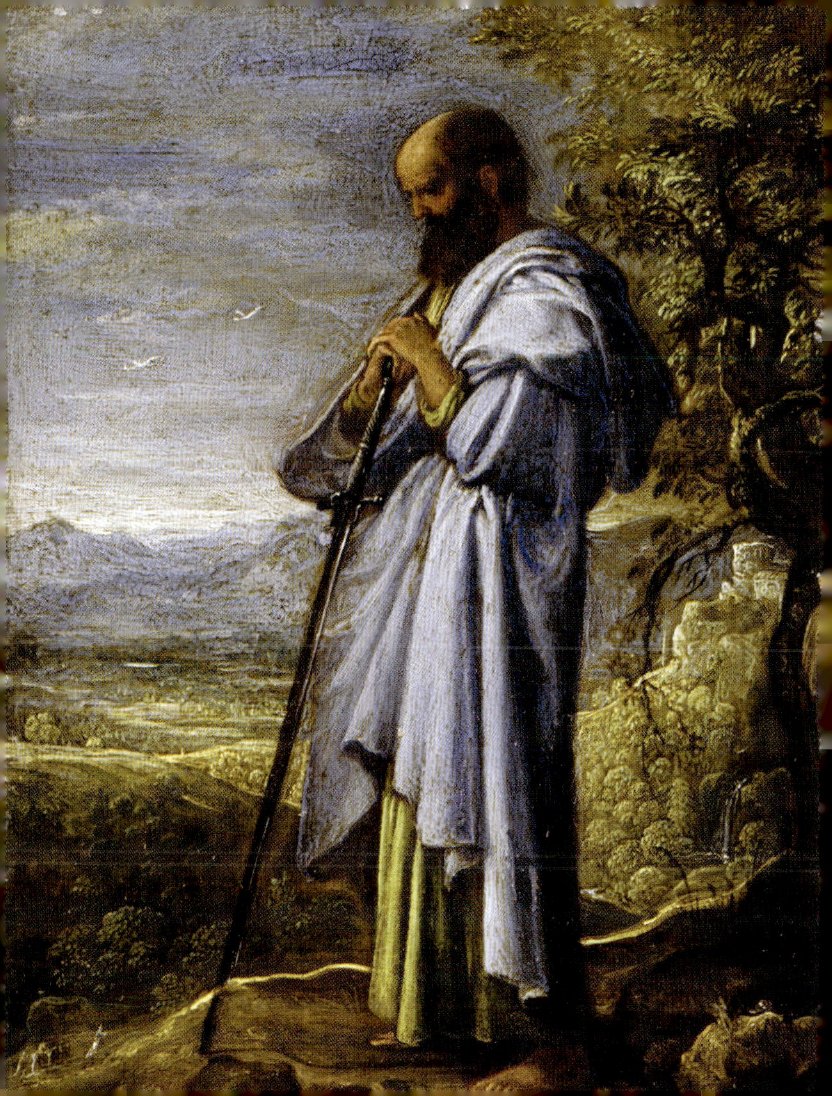

it the respect of the great' – a clear indication of his passionate concern with the status of the artist and his social role. Baglione's approach is relatively straightforward, factual, and annalistic, without Bellori's concern with selection or theoretical framework; he claims in his introduction to look for 'the clarity of truth'. Like Rubens in his letter to Faber, Baglione speaks first of Elsheimer's mastery of 'small figures', praising the gratia *with which they were painted; then the 'beautiful landscapes', painted* del vivo *– significantly commenting on the way the figures 'accord' with the landscape, resulting in 'miraculous harmony'. Baglione attributes Elsheimer's failure to complete his work to an excessive perfectionism, and his death to a stomach illness caused by the strain of his work, and consequent exhaustion. He is the only biographer to comment on Elsheimer's good looks and 'noble presence', again revealing his concern with the artist as gentleman and* virtuoso. *The only work singled out by Baglione is, again, a 'night piece', in this case a print of 'a Sorceress'; presumably a print after the early* Witch *– a piece which accords with a certain taste for the macabre at the time (most famously expressed by Salvator Rosa), reminding us that witch-trials were a common occurrence. Baglione, as proud member of the Accademia di S. Luca, ends by referring to the artist's self-portrait then exhibited there (Florence, Uffizi).*

The longest and most substantial biography is that by Joachim von Sandrart (1606-88), German artist and antiquarian, from Frankfurt like Elsheimer, who was in Rome from 1629 to 1635, meeting a number of artists, and from 1632 lodging in the Giustiniani household. Though Elsheimer had been dead for 19 years when Sandrart was in Rome, he states that he met the artist's widow. Sandrart is now known chiefly for his book entitled Academia Todesca della architectura, scultura e pittura Oder Teutsche Academie, *published in 1675-79; a Latin edition appeared in 1683. This volume contains engravings after Roman antiquities as well as biographies of artists, but the most original part is that devoted to lives of recent or contemporary Northern artists; it is valuable also for the (occasionally rather boastful) accounts of artistic life in Rome in the 1630s, when Sandrart went sketching in the Roman Campagna with Claude and Poussin. The* Life *of Elsheimer is more detailed than those by Mancini or Baglione and is an invaluable source– though not necessarily always accurate (he states that Elsheimer had several children, whereas in fact there was only one son).*

In Sandrart's biography, praise of Elsheimer's naturalism is a constant motif, perhaps reflecting his Northern

Overleaf: Aurora, c. 1606.

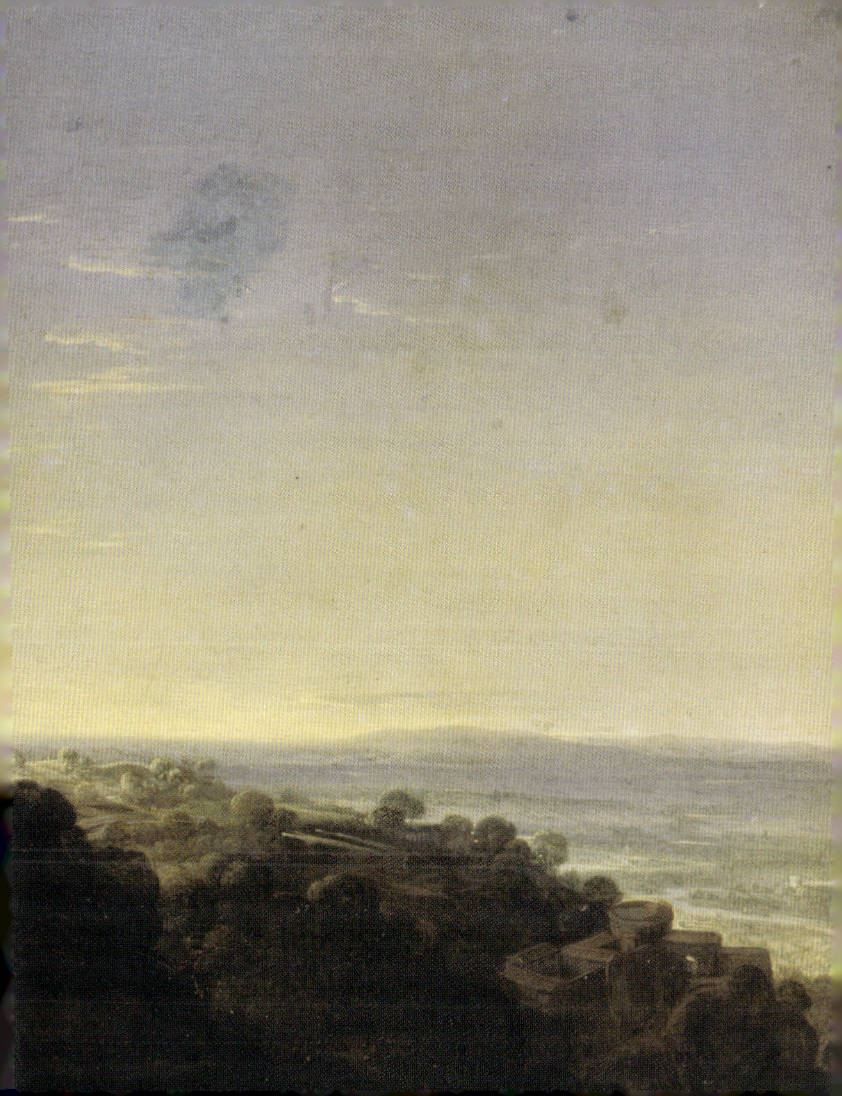

orientation; the artist is described as 'the first to paint small pictures of landscapes', acting as a model for other painters as 'the most perfect, the most select and the most natural'. In this context, he singles out the Small Tobias *(Frankfurt, Historisches Museum) as having created a sensation in Rome; he praises particularly the morning sunlight and the 'beautiful' landscape, again stressing the 'natural' and lifelike qualities of the work. He praises, too, the contrast of dawn sky and dark hill, as well as the extensive vista stretching to the horizon, and 'marvellous colouring' in the* Aurora *(Braunschweig, Herzog Anton Ulrich Museum) (its title derives from Goudt's engraving – Sandrart is not aware that originally the artist planned the subject of Acis and Galatea, with the Cyclops Polyphemus.) This work, with its bold simplicity of form and subtle use of ærial and tonal gradation, suggests some of Claude's atmospheric effects.*

While Sandrart constantly praises Elsheimer's naturalism, he also commends the 'poetry, invention and imagination' of Il Contento, *which he considers the artist's greatest work, though he does not appear to realize that it is unfinished, or that the subject is taken from a Spanish picaresque novel. This highly complex and unusual composition – for which, exceptionally, preparatory drawings survive – is praised for its 'original and curious manner', as well as for the way in which the crowds are 'marvellously illuminated'.*

Sandrart, like Van Mander and Baglione, is particularly fascinated by a group of 'night pieces', including the interior scene, Jupiter and Baucis in the Home of Philemon and Baucis, *which, with* The Mocking of Ceres, *is held up as a 'school' for painting 'darkness', from which Sandrart had himself learned in his youth. The artist's tour de force as a study of nocturnal and artificial lighting, the* Flight into Egypt, *which was in his studio at the time of his death, is described as 'incomparable' for its rendering of the Milky Way as a stream of stars, and the moon with its answering reflection. Sandrart claims 'often' to have been shown the original painting by Goudt, whose engraving he compares with it unfavourably . It seems likely that Elsheimer was aware of contemporary astronomical researches, even though Galileo's writings were published a year later (1610); he was in touch with Cesi, the founder of the scientific Accademia dei Lincei, who belonged to Faber's circle.*

Like Van Mander, Sandrart emphasizes the vividness

Overleaf: copy after the 'Large Tobias', c. 1607-8.

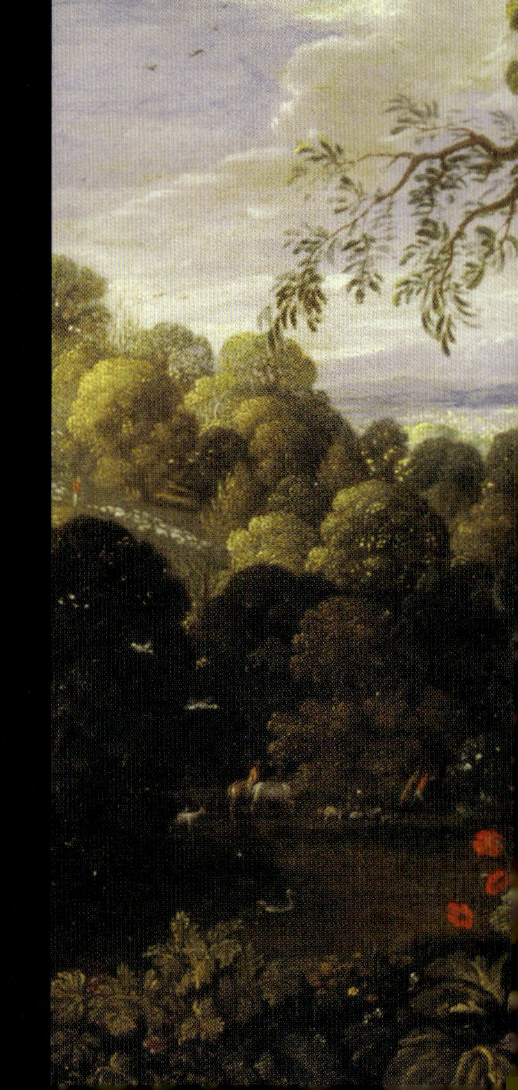

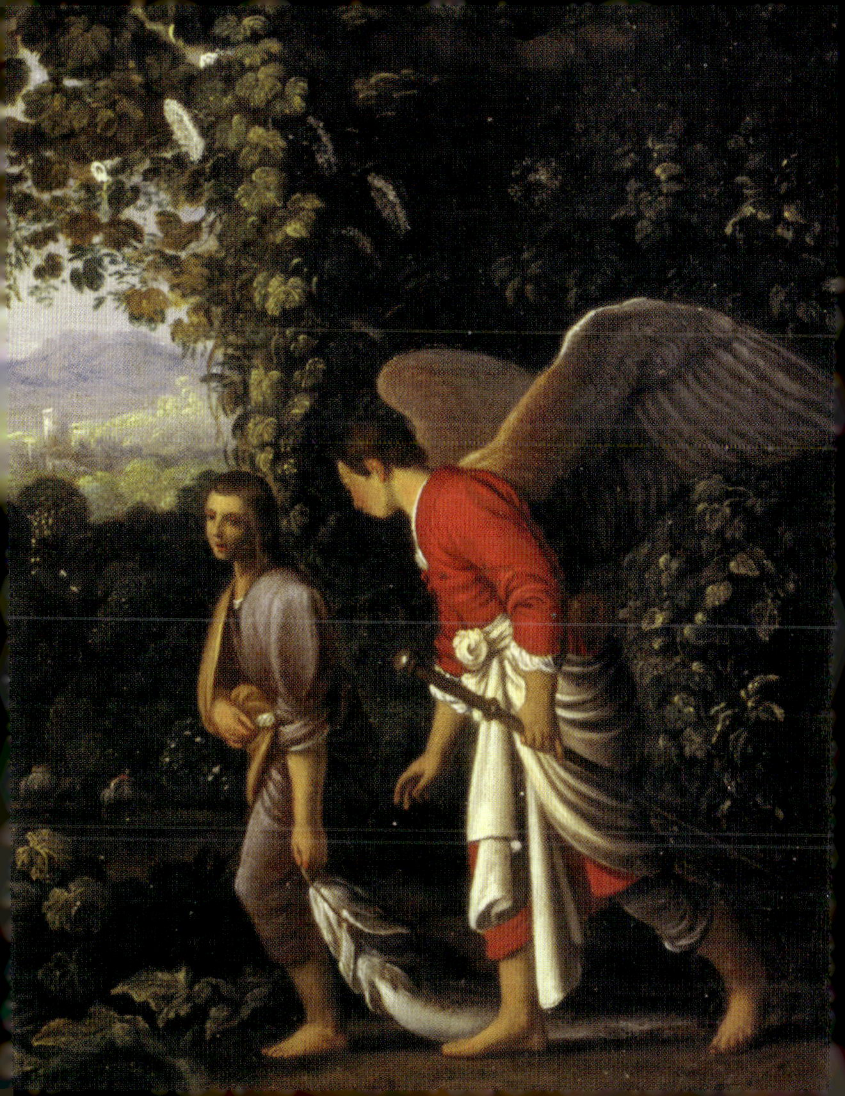

of Elsheimer's visual memory, suggesting that he would spend hours contemplating nature, in such sites as the Vigna Madama, and did not need drawings to record his impressions. This intensity of observation resulted in unusually precise renderings of natural forms, such as particular species of tree, but also – Sandrart suggests – led to his final state of exhaustion and depression. The rendering of the luxuriant vegetation in the Large Tobias *(lost, but known by engravings and copies) may exemplify this vividly precise observation of nature. His biography ends with a renewed tribute to Elsheimer's 'perfect draughtsmanship and natural colouring', as well as suggesting the calm monumentality of his figures, in a reference to his avoidance of 'fleeting movement', and deploring the fact that Frankfurt – his own native city as well as that of Elsheimer – did not own a single work by the artist.*

The last, brief, biography printed here was written over a century after Sandrart, by the French dealer, painter and collector J. B. P. Le Brun (1746-1813), great-nephew of Charles Le Brun, and husband of Elisabeth Vigée Le Brun. He acted as Louis XVI's agent at art sales, and was intermediary for foreign collectors, including Catherine the Great.

In his Galerie des peintres flamands, hollandais &

allemands *(1792-6) Le Brun expressed real enthusiasm for Northern European art. His biography of Elsheimer reflects his dominant interests as a leading connoisseur and dealer, with a concern for the technical and æsthetic qualities of the works, noting the state of preservation of the paintings. In particular, he comments on their monetary value, recording the high prices that they fetched. Pointing to the number of copies and imitations, Le Brun concludes that 'real connoisseurship and careful examination' are needed to distinguish copies from originals.*

The early biographies, while differing in emphasis, single out some of the qualities in Elsheimer's art which we admire today: the amazingly fine detail, the mastery of composition and figure drawing on a minute scale, the depiction of landscape, and especially the rendering of different effects of nocturnal and artificial lighting. While Rubens and Rembrandt were drawn to Elsheimer's skill as a narrative painter, for us the summit of his achievement perhaps lies in the marvellous fusion of figures and landscape in the creation of a particular mood – evident for instance, in the pristine setting of the Small Tobias, *with its softly rounded trees and intimation of early morning light. But nowhere is this more evident than in his celebrated* Flight into Egypt, *so coveted by Rubens, where the different light sources – the fire, the torch, the stars of the Milky Way, and the serene moonlight – illuminate the passage of the Holy Family by night. The stars and moon may be symbolic of the Virgin mother, or of divine majesty, and their accurate depiction may reflect recent astronomical discoveries; in any case they combine to create a magical and mysterious world, in which figures and setting join in 'miraculous harmony', in Baglione's words.*

CAREL VAN MANDER

The Life of Adam Elsheimer

from

Het Leven der Doorluchtighe Nederlandtsche en Hooghduytsche Schilders

1604

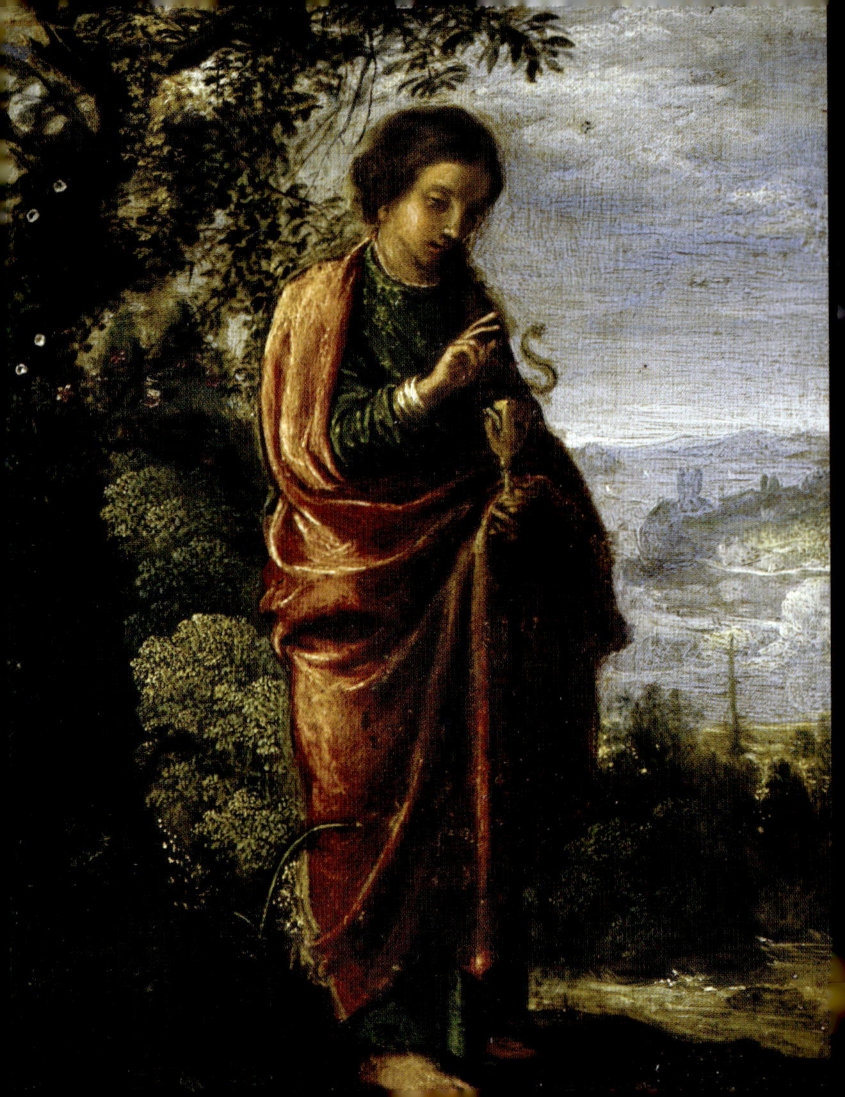

At the moment there still lives in Rome an excellent German painter called Adam, who was born in Frankfurt, the son of a tailor. When he came to Italy his skill in painting was still rather poor, but in Rome he made amazing progress and through hard work became a skilled craftsman. He does not busy himself particularly with drawing, but rather sits in churches or elsewhere in order to look at the works of the great masters, impressing everything securely in his memory. He knows amazingly well how to paint his inventions on to copper plates and although he is not very productive, he does it excellently well. He is good-natured and obliging to everyone. In this year 1604, he is about 28 or 30 years old.

Opposite: St. John the Evangelist, c. 1605. This painting is one of at least ten small panels probably intended for a piece of devotional furniture. Nine survive, and four more are reproduced: overleaf (John the Baptist) and on pp. 25, 42 and 86

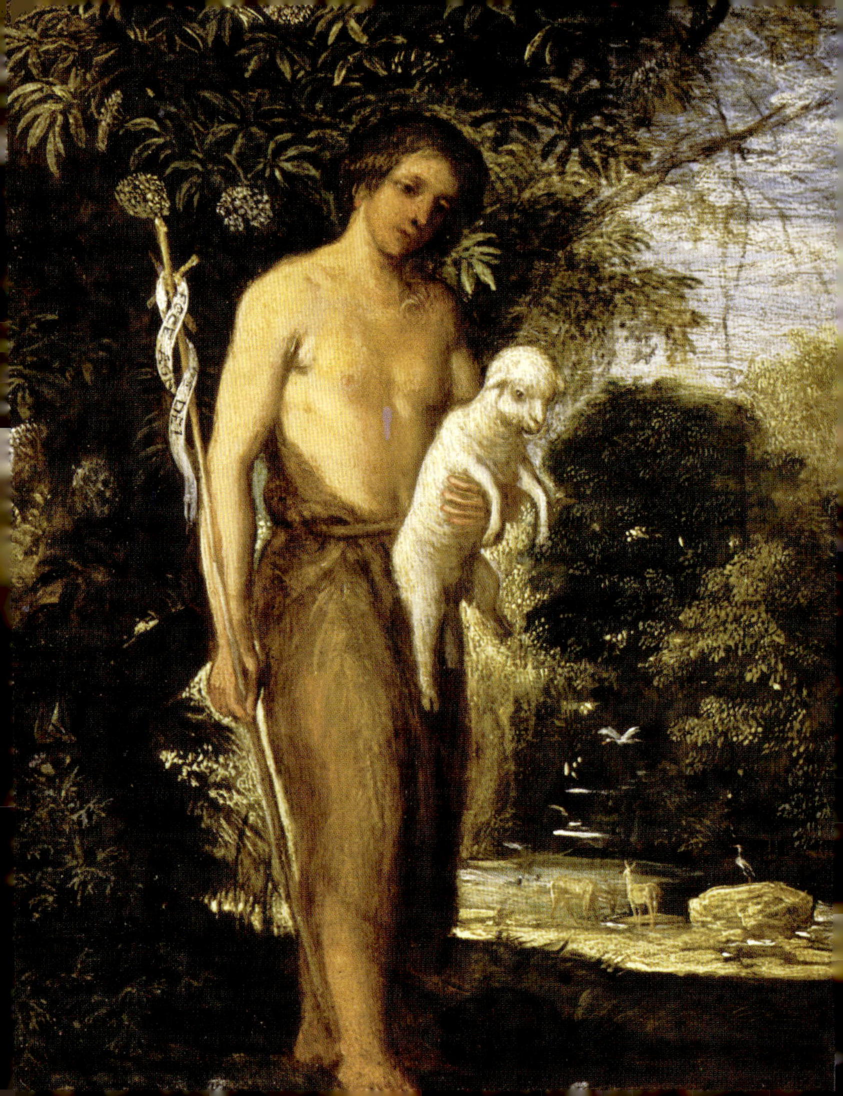
DEI

GIULIO MANCINI

Life of Adam Elsheimer

from the
Considerazioni sulla Pittura

c. 1614-21

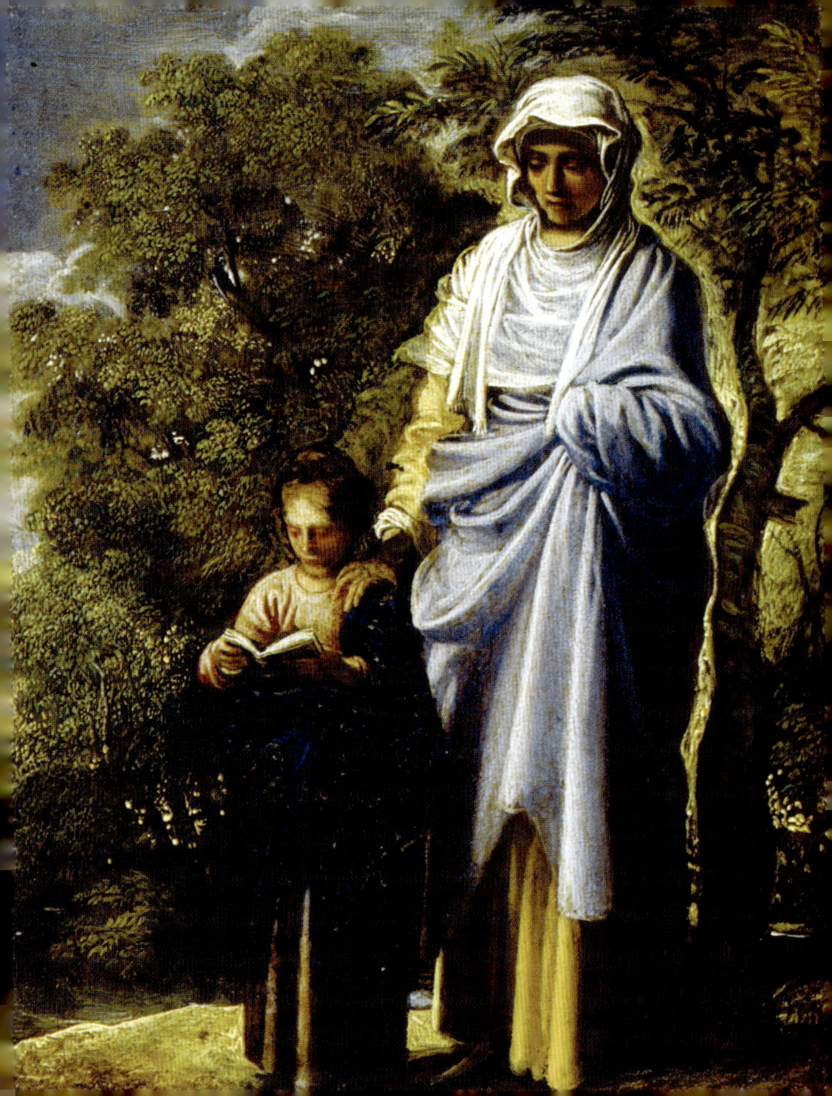

He came to Rome from Germany about the year 1600 and, working with Italian painters, quickly adopted their manner. He worked on a small scale with such design, finish, colour and grace that it is marvellous, particularly in night-pieces.

One sees little of his work because he produced little and this little is in the hands of princes and those persons who, in order that they should not be taken from them, keep them hidden. Some of his works were engraved by the Cavaliere ***, his great friend, with whom however he had a quarrel. During his illness they became reconciled and this Cavalier behaved like the greatest of friends.

He died recently to the great sorrow and shock of those of his profession who knew him. He was buried with great honours by his countrymen, and accompanied to his grave by the painters of the Academy.

Opposite: The Education of the Virgin, c. 1605.

Overleaf: The Finding and the Exaltation of the True Cross, now known as The Frankfurt Tabernacle, c. 1603-5. The central painting is shown on p. 46, and two subsidiary panel on pp. 48-49.

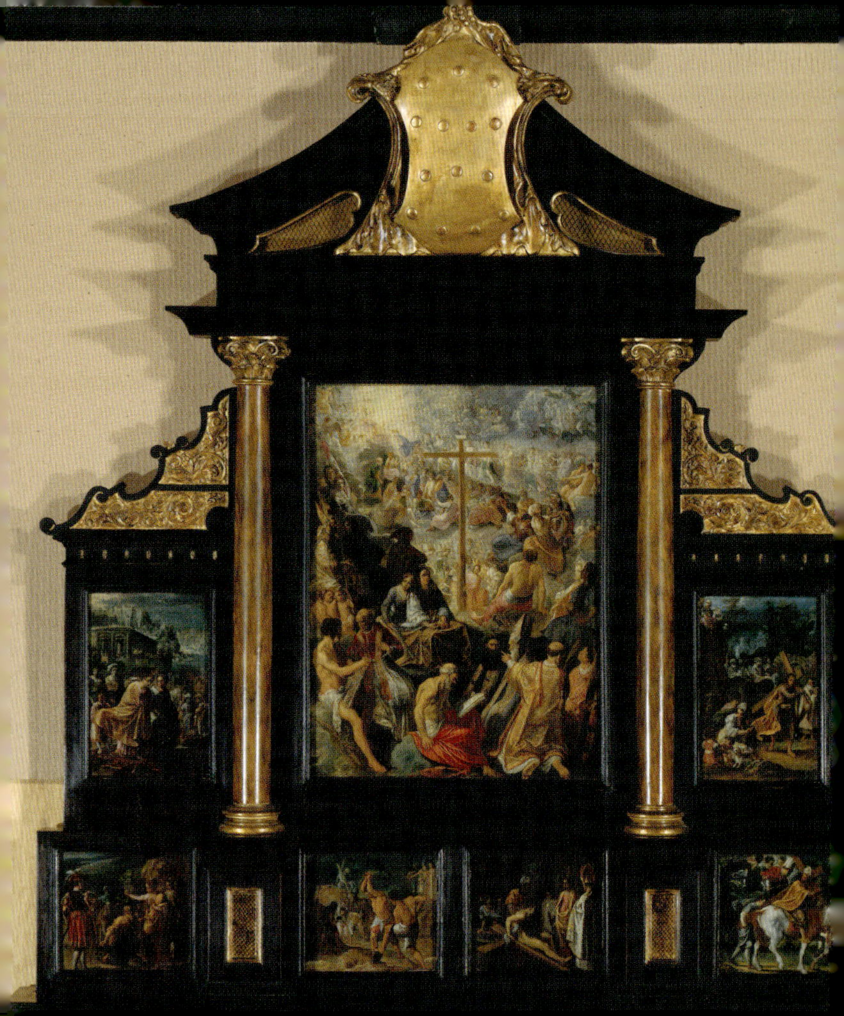

JUSEPE MARTINEZ

A visit to Elsheimer's Glory

from
Discursos practicables
del nobilissimo Arte
de la Pintura

c. 1670

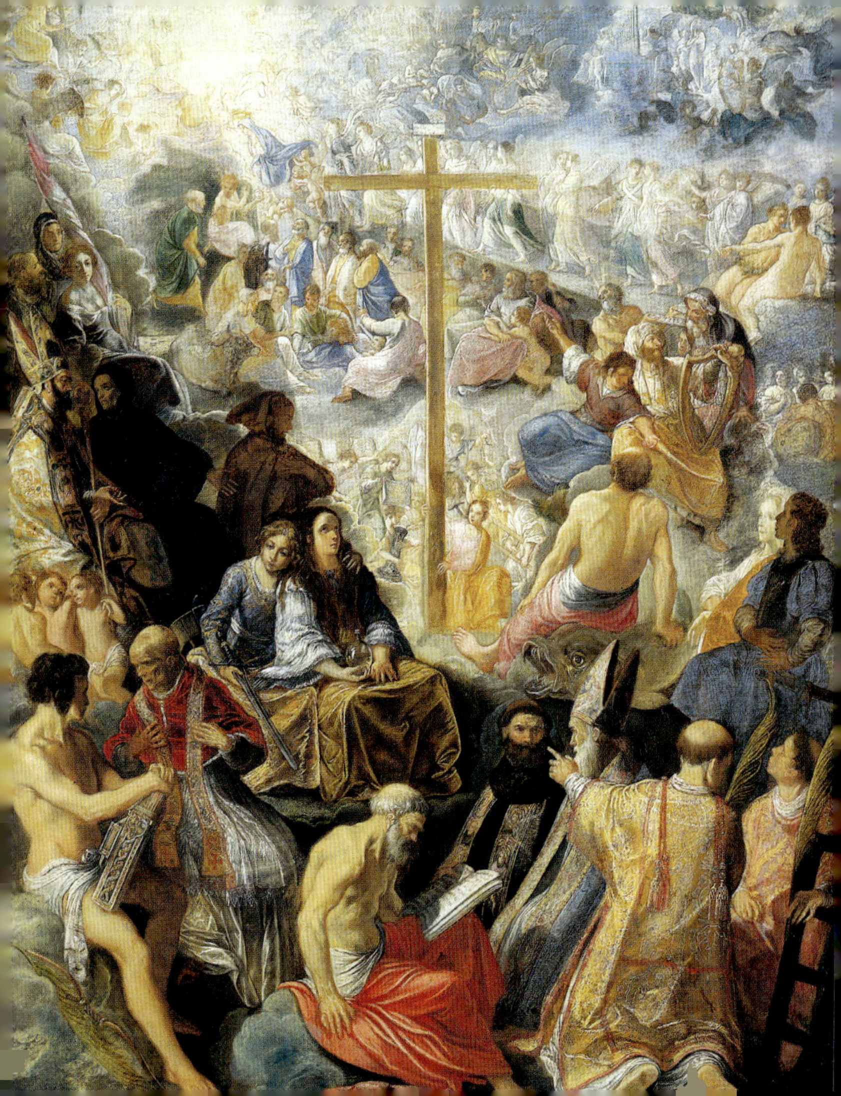

At a certain occasion, it happened that I visited a palace among the entourage of a great painter [never identified, but a friend of Reni and Domenichino], where we were shown a painting, representing a *Glory*, with a multitude of figures, with so much expression, dignity and skilful contrasts, that it amazed both connoisseurs and laymen. The great painter, who had taken me with him for the inspection, was asked what he thought of it (for it was for this purpose that he had been called). He answered that the painting was so excellent and so well thought out that he believed nothing could be better made. It was certain that if the figures were to be enlarged to natural size, it would outshine all previous paintings.

The painting is from the hand of a Flemish painter who had studied in Rome for fifteen years, called Adam del Samar. The figures of this painter do not exceed a 'tercia'. He was of a very hermit-like

Opposite: The Exaltation of the True Cross c. 1603-5. This is possibly the painting that Martinez visited in the 1620's, and described as a 'Glory'. It is part of an altarpiece now known as 'The Frankfurt Tabernacle', which is reproduced on p. 42; two more of the panels are reproduced overleaf: The Empress Helena embarking to find the True Cross, left, and The Emperor Heraclius carrying the Cross into Jerusalem, right

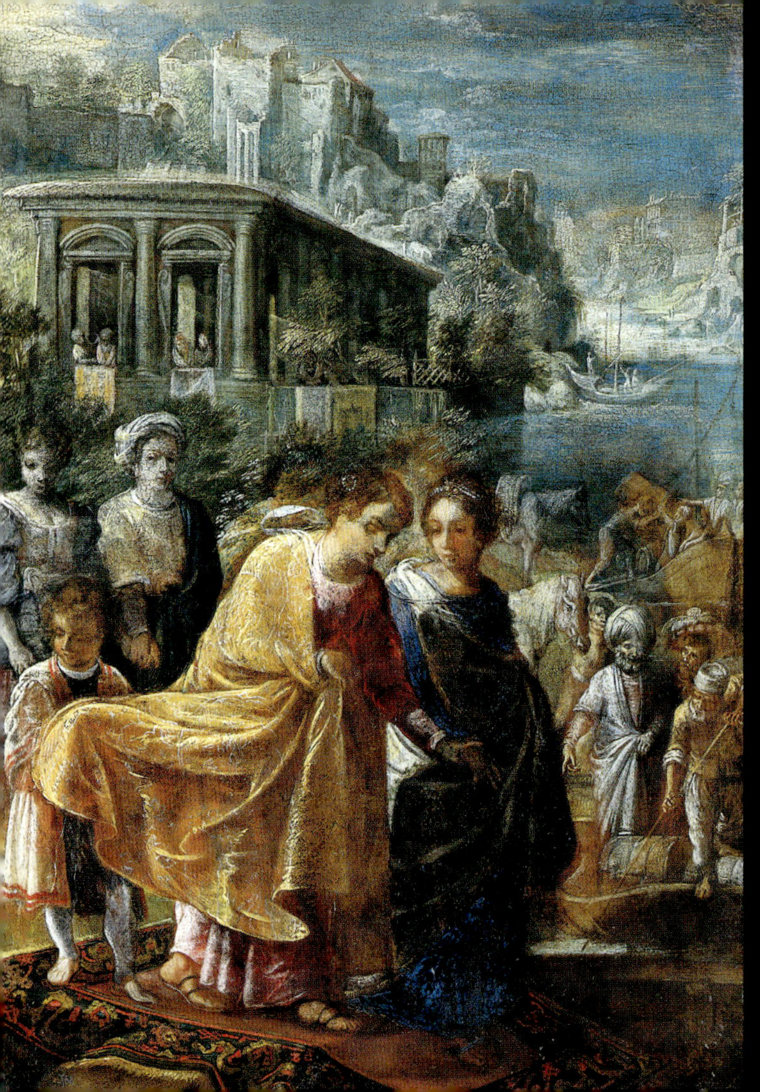

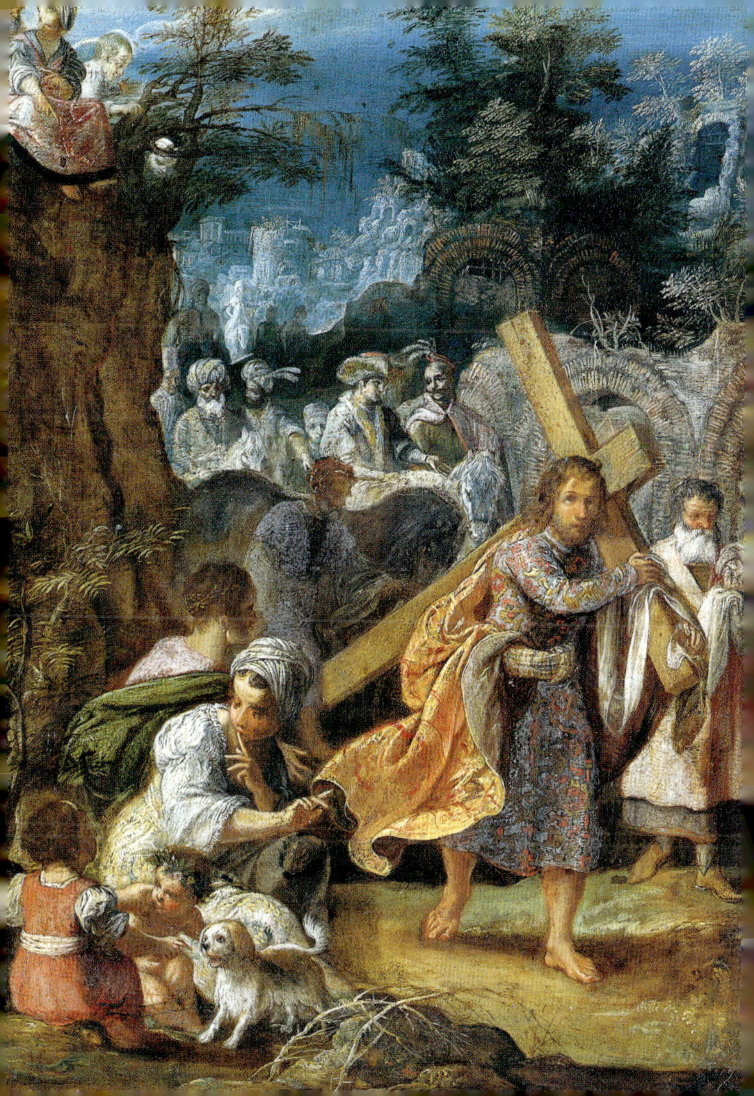

and meditative nature and walked along the streets so rapt in contemplation that he did not speak to anyone who addressed him. He judged himself a lesser artist than he in fact was; his friends remonstrated with him to change his manner, by putting more trust in himself, which was his due. His answer always was, that when he himself was satisfied with his works he would heed their advice.

JOHANN FABER

'The Mocking of Ceres'

from the
Animalia Mexicana
descriptionibus
scholiisque exposita

c. 1628

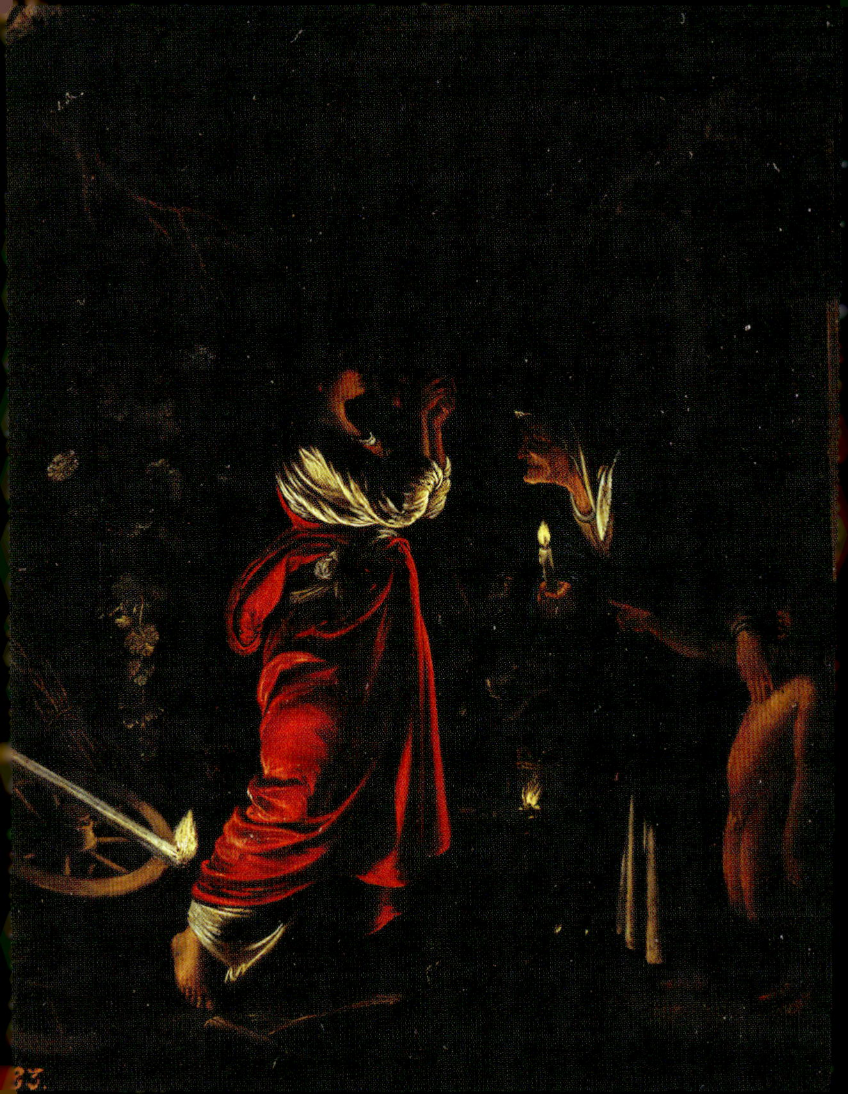
83.

Even if asked to judge, I shall be loath to give my verdict on who has provided the more elegant version of this tale – Ovid, that most eloquent poet, or Adam Elsheimer of Frankfurt, once a regular guest in my house, with his most charming painting. He painted this story on a copper plate one and a half spans long and one wide, with such skill and artistry, such learning and talent and allowed it thereafter to be engraved on copper, that no comparable work of art had ever been seen at Rome and on that account it was sold for more than two hundred gold Philippes. Here, where small figures had to be represented as though living and breathing, and at night-time too, or at sunrise or sunset, where rain-showers, tides or some such natural phenomenon had to be depicted and painted, he took the palm above all painters of his time. In rendering the charm of woods and trees,

Opposite: The Mocking of Ceres, c. 1608. Ovid tells how Ceres, searching for her abducted daughter Proserpine, arrives at the hut of an old woman and asks for water. While she drinks greedily, she is mocked by the young boy Stellio, whom she angrily transforms into a lizard. Faber's account of this painting is inserted in his description of the Mexican lizard 'Stellio Novæ Hispaniæ'. The original painting, now in Milwaukee, Dr. Alfred Bader collection, is badly damaged; the illustration here is of the old copy at the Prado, Madrid, which once belonged to Rubens

the beauty of flowers, the pleasures of the countryside in living colour, he so captured the true essence of nature that he opened the eyes of painters not only of his own day but (in this matter especially) of those too who came after. Only the late Paul Bril of Belgium, a painter of great distinction at Rome, could teach this. After he followed Adam's manner, in these last twenty years of his life, he left us works in this kind of painting (the Italians call them '*paesi*') which are really golden; but those which he himself gave to the world before these twenty years are of bronze (if I may say so), although he was famous even then. But, these are only words, you will say. So I invite you to view Adam's works themselves; I have some, though only a few, at home.

GIOVANNI BAGLIONE

The Life of Adam Elsheimer, Painter

from
Le Vite de' Pittori, Scultori, Architetti, ed Intagliatori dal Pontificato di Gregorio XIII. *del 1572. fino a tempi di Papa Urbano* VIII. *nel 1642.*

1642

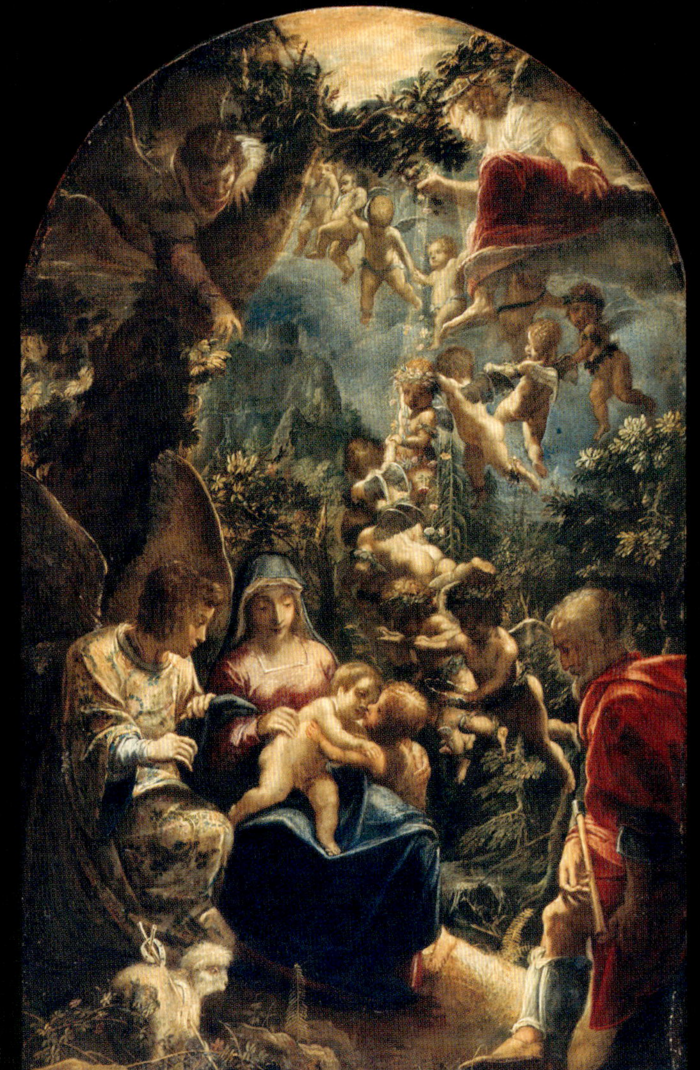

They say that the palm grows upwards even under a weight; but ability under strain sometimes fails, and strength cannot withstand force if it is not refreshed by rest.

During this period [i.e. the Pontificate of Paul V] there was Adam of Frankfurt, the German. This was the excellent painter of small figures which he had rendered with the greatest skill and mastery. These he created with great taste, good design and rare invention, and with such delicacy and vividness, so that he could be compared with any painter.

And on this small scale he also painted such beautiful landscapes which, being taken from nature, accorded with these figures – all vividly painted and producing a miraculous harmony.

Eager to perfect his works, he took a long time over them, thus often leaving incomplete his work and with it his profit: these are all the signs that in work the companion of ability must be honour. One does not see his works in public, because he painted

Opposite: The Holy Family with the Infant St. John, c. 1599.
Overleaf: The Burning of Troy, c. 1600-01

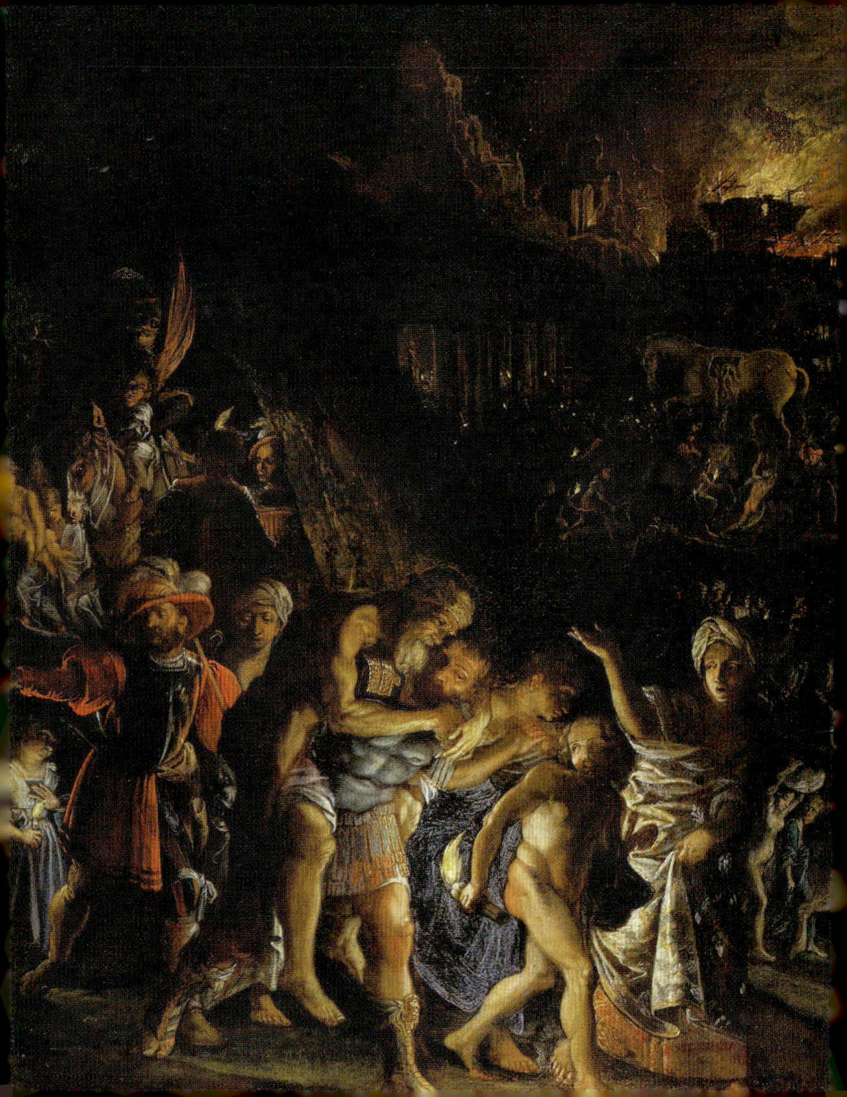

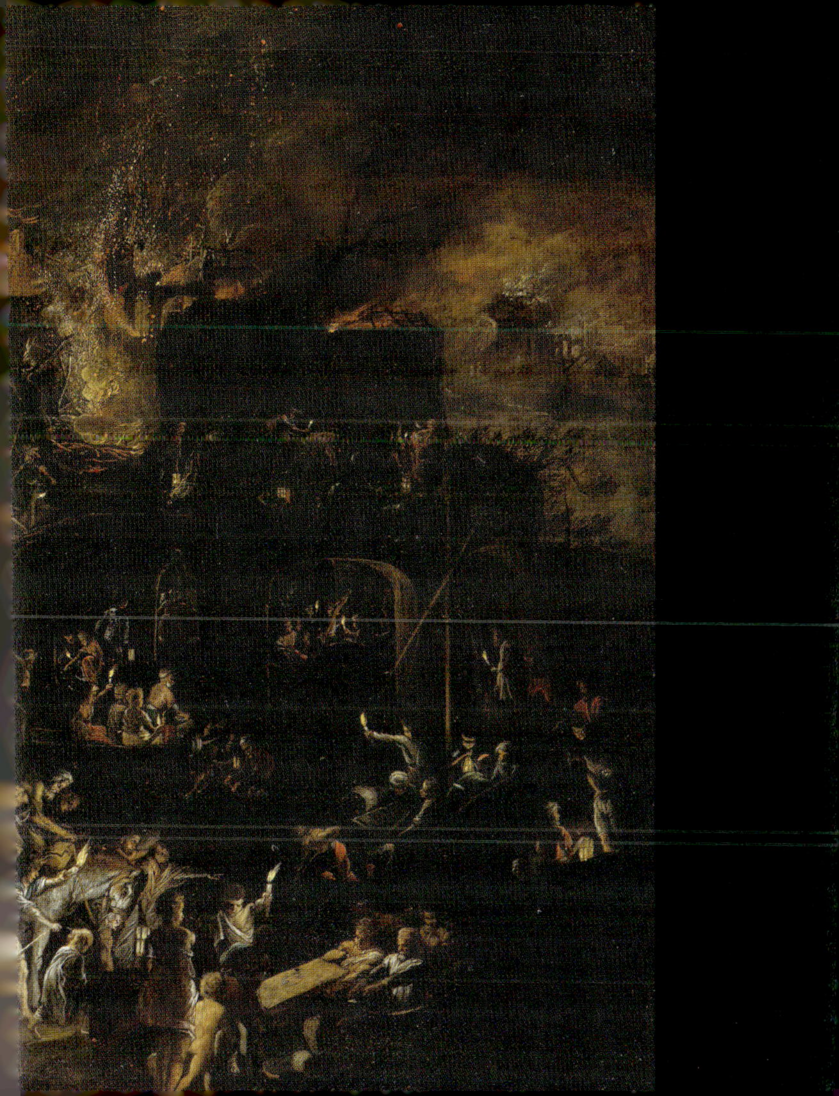

little, and in such a size that in any public exhibition they would have remained unnoticed.

It was a great loss to lose such a man so early, since he would have left some excellent works (though small ones) as evidence of his ability.

He died young of a stomach complaint, it is said, caused by painting so many small pieces with so much effort; in his efforts to bring his talents to fruition, he declined in the prime of his life, and died of exhaustion.

He was a good-looking man and of noble presence. He was married to a Scotch lady, and in order to be able to live in comfort, the Apostolic Palace administered to them a reasonable subsistence.

I once saw a print depicting a night-piece with a Sorceress and with all kinds of spells which represented the horrors of the underworld, and the terrors of the magic arts – a work so beautiful as other works of his have been found to be.

Opposite: The Witch, c. 1596-7. Baglione is probably referring to a print after this painting

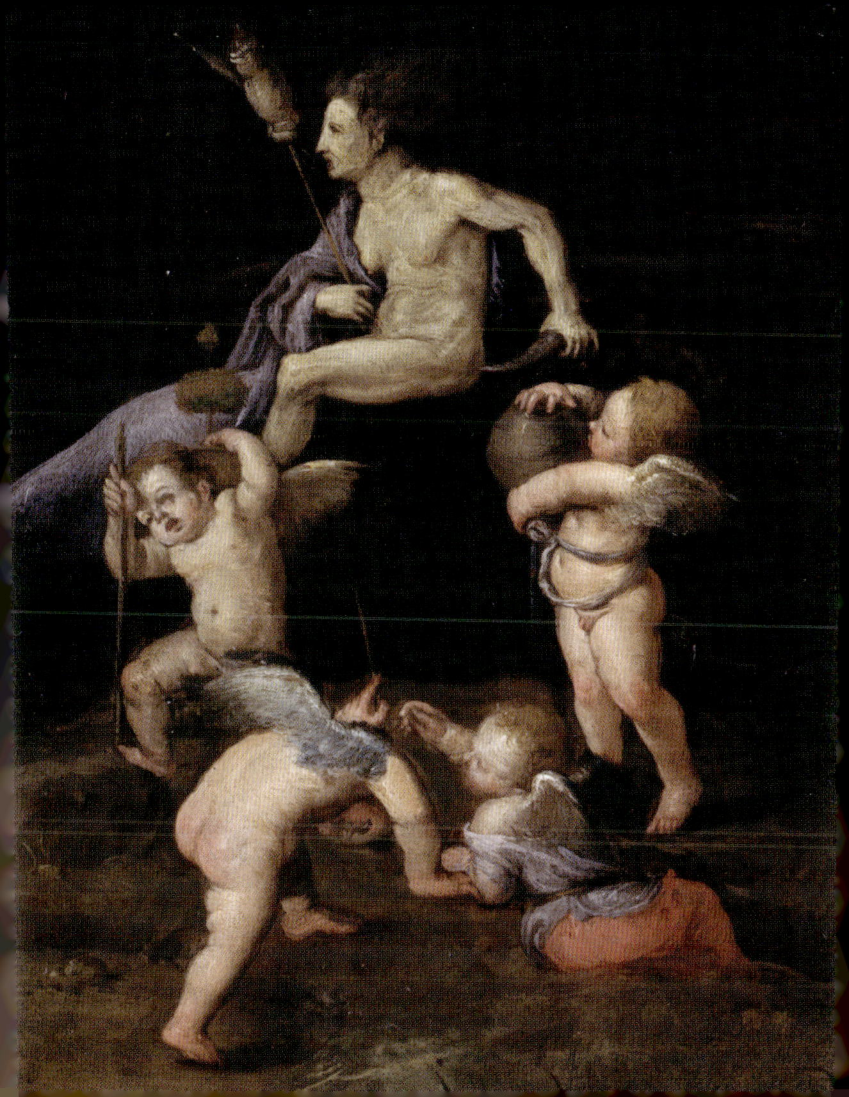

He died in my native town, during the Pontificate of Paul V; and his portrait[1] can be seen in the Accademia di S. Luca, to perpetuate his memory.

1. Florence, Uffizi

JOACHIM VON SANDRART

The Life of Adam Elsheimer, Painter

from

Teutsche Akademie der Bau-, Bild- und Mahlerey-Künste

1675

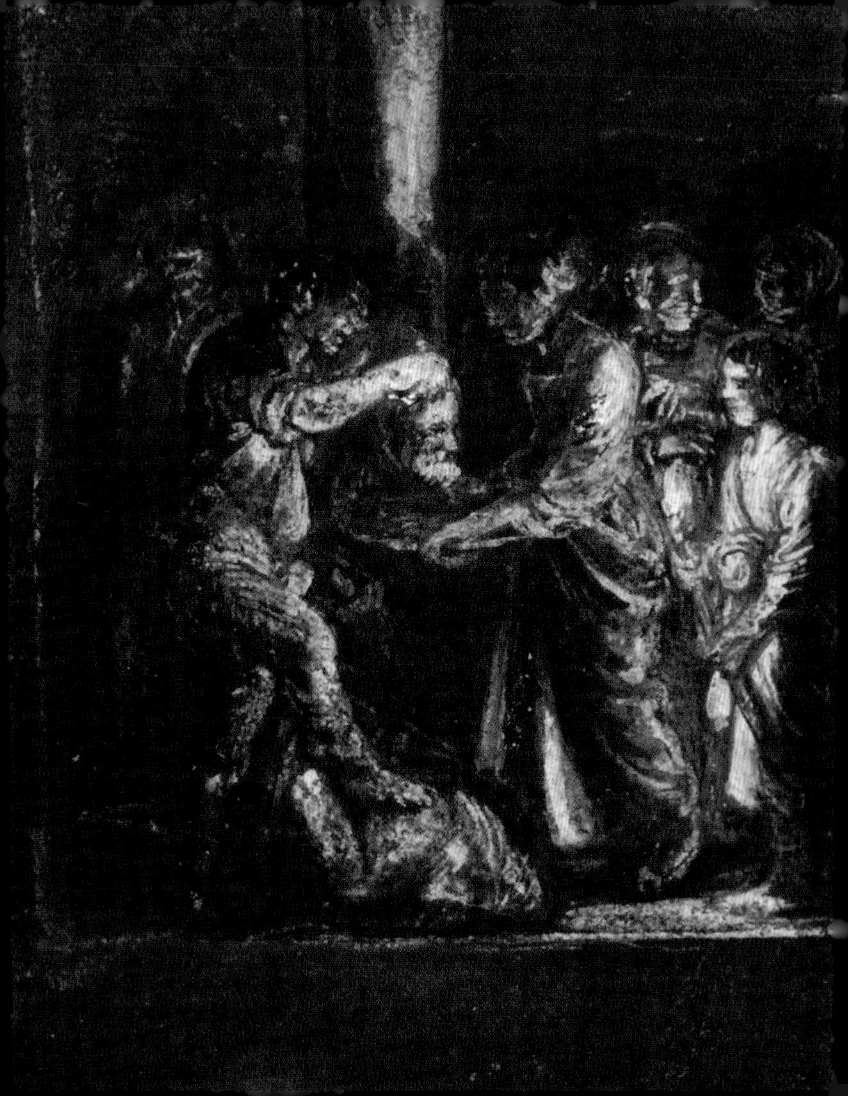

One of the most famous and highly praised masters in the noble art of painting was Adam Elsheimer, generally called Adam of Frankfurt, the son of a tailor, bom in Frankfurt next to the 'Rothe Badstuben' in the year 1574. Because he felt a great urge to paint he began to draw and subsequently went to study with Philipp Uffenbach. Because he aimed at greatest perfection he soon travelled through Germany in order to get to Rome. This he managed to do and there he joined the most virtuous and famous. Among those who found themselves there, in order to gain the highest peak of perfection, were such different painters as Pieter Lastman, Jan Pynas of Amsterdam and Jacob Ernst Thoman of Lindau, and others. just as our forefather Adam was the first man, so this Adam was the first to paint small pictures of landscapes and other curiosities in which he reached such heights that he became a predecessor and father whose manner has been imitated in all regions by all other painters as being the most perfect, the most select and the most natural.

Opposite: Beheading of John the Baptist

Overleaf: The 'Small Tobias', c. 1607-8.

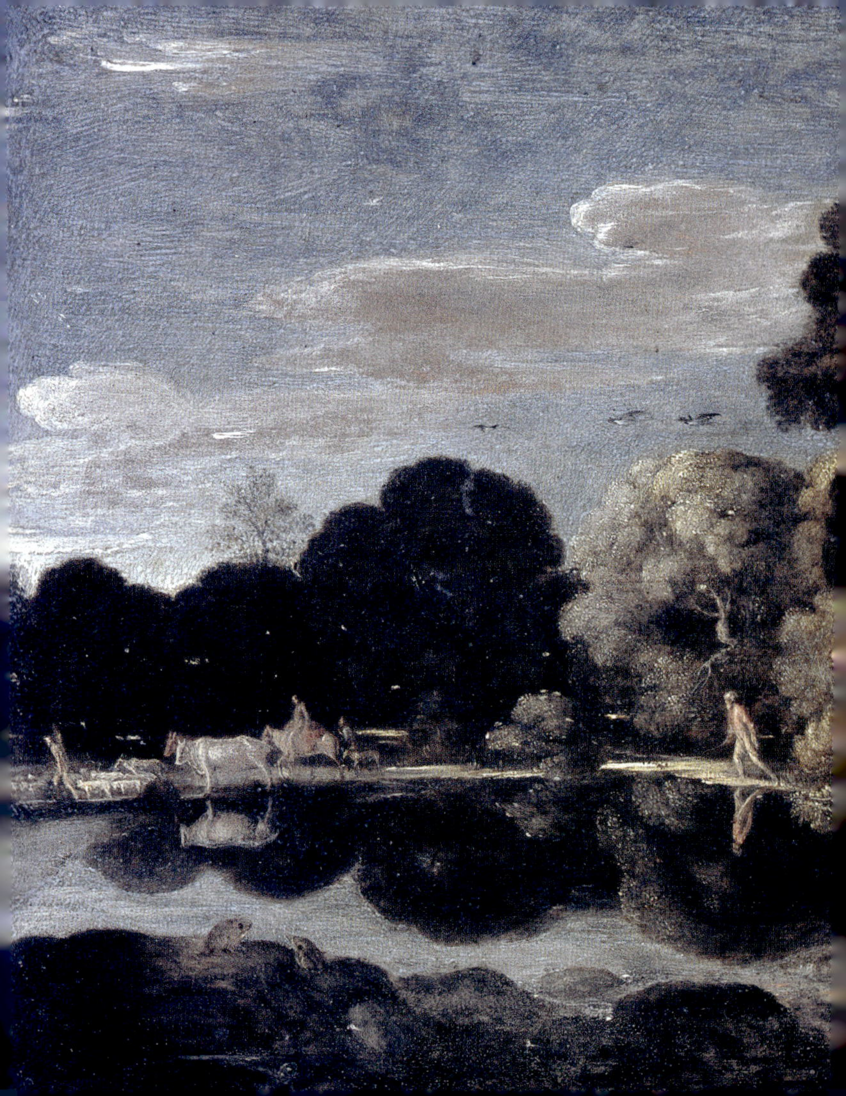

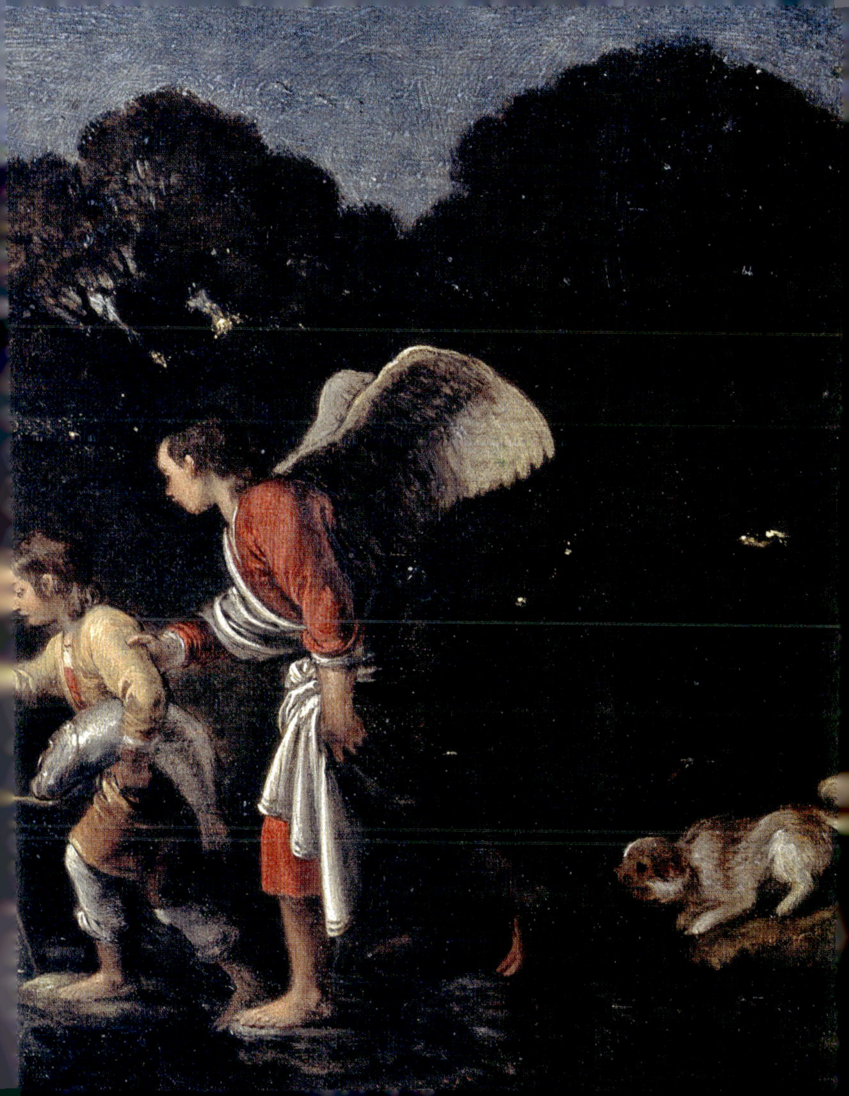

Among his best works which increased his reputation was a small *Tobias*[1] painted on a little copperplate the width of a hand in which the angel helps the young Tobias to traverse a shallow brook, whilst a little dog jumps from one stone to the next eager to catch up with them. Both are illuminated by the bright rising sun. The landscape is so beautiful, the reflection of the sky in the water so natural, the travellers and animals so well rendered, that nothing like it has ever been seen before and hence the whole of Rome talked about nothing but of Elsheimer's newly discovered art of painting in the same manner he painted a slightly larger landscape with Latona and the two children,[2] to whom the peasants, working in the bog, begrudge the clear water for drinking, because of which they are being changed into frogs. Furthermore, he painted in the same size the wounded and naked Procris, whom Cephalus tries to save through healing herbs.[3] In the distance are field-goddesses, satyrs, fauns, old and young, who kindle a fire in front of the wood. No less skilful is his

1. Frankfurt, Historisches Museum 2. Cologne, Wallraf-Richartz Museum 3. Liverpool, National Museums; the subject is in fact Apollo and Coronis

Opposite: Apollo and Coronis, c. 1607-8.

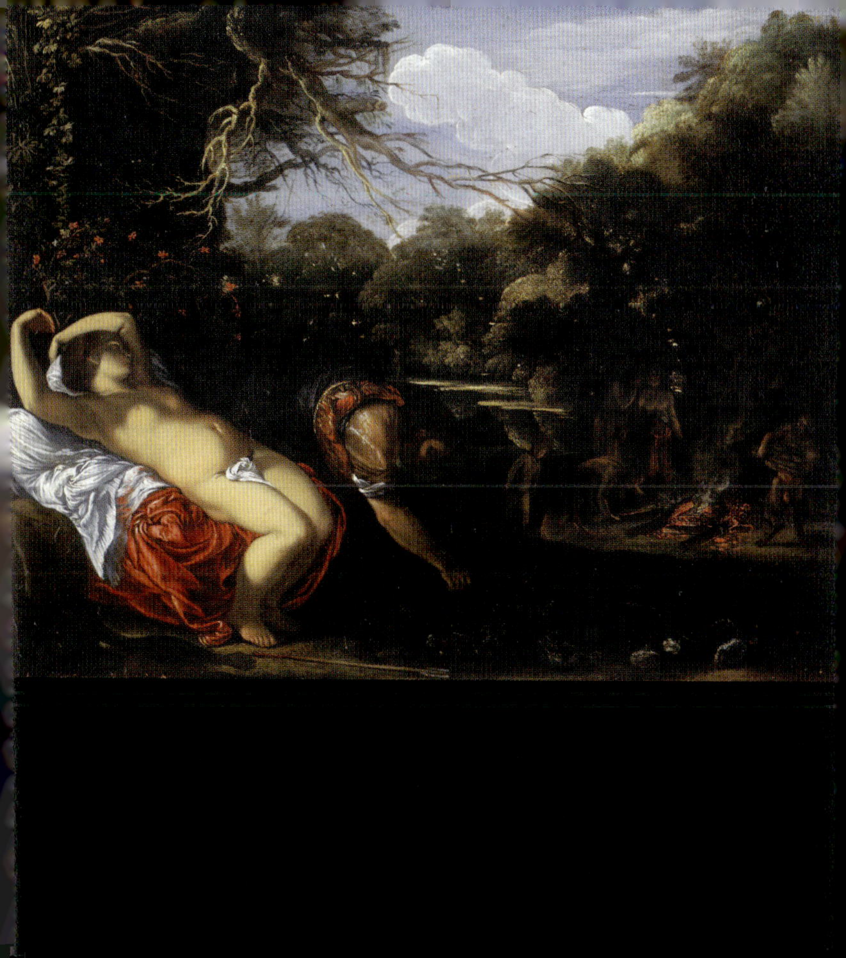

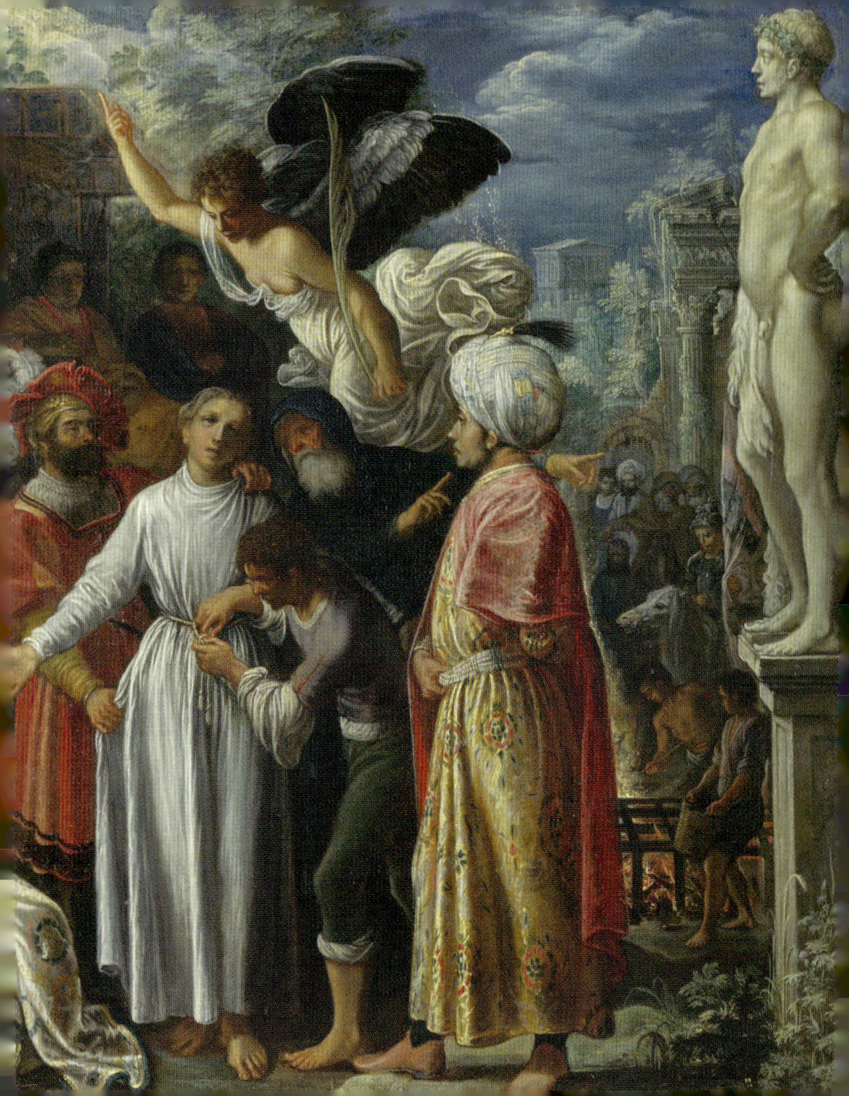

painting of St. Lawrence, who, being disrobed before the judge before being roasted on the gridiron in front of the pagan god, turns his gaze to heaven.[1] This is an indescribably moving work, of which the original can now be seen in the residence of Count Johann von Nassau at Saarbrücken amongst many other rarities. He also painted another small St. Lawrence[2] for my cousin Abraham Mertens of Frankfurt, in which the figure is seen clad in a highly wrought chasuble, in one hand the gridiron, in the other the palm branch, in the background a wide vista with mountains, valleys, waterfalls, tiny buildings all illuminated by the evening sun. The whole is so naturally and imaginatively rendered that I lack words rather than matter to praise it adequately. After this much admired, newly acquired way to paint in oil on a small scale, he abandoned painting on a large scale (which was his first manner) and continued painting small.

He also etched several small landscapes in which field-gods and nymphs dance with cymbals, and satyrs make music and other equally clever curiosities.

1. London, National Gallery 2. Montpellier, Musée Fabre; illustrated p. 86

Opposite: St. Lawrence Being Prepared for Martyrdom, c. 1600-1.

Furthermore, he painted an Aurora[1] against a dark wood with a view over distant mountains and valleys to the horizon – all marvellously coloured. Again in small oval form the decapitation of St. John the Baptist[2] in which he showed his great skill in the only true method of painting night pieces. This was subsequently so highly praised that, stimulated by it, he painted also the story of how Jupiter and Mercury arrived, tired from a long journey, in the poor peasant hut of Baucis and Philemon.[3] They had sat down and were illuminated, like the two poor people and their utensils, from the light of lamps, in such a manner that this and the following work became a school and lesson from which one could learn how to paint darkness properly, and I admit that I myself in my youth took these works for my guideline and pattern when I started to paint night pieces. Equally skilful is the great work of Ceres drinking by night whilst she is standing by an old woman with a candle and is being mocked by an impudent boy.[4] This work deserves the highest praise partly because of its marvellous design and invention, partly because of

1. Braunschweig, Herzog Anton-Ulrich Museum, illustrated p. 28. 2. A related gouache is at Chatsworth, illustrated p. 64. 3. Dresden, Staatliche Kunstsamm-lungen 4. Milwaukee, Dr. Alfred Bader; copy in Madrid, Prado, illustrated p. 52.

the drawing, the colour and the different beautiful lights, the landscape and trees as well as the hanging foliage, leaves and ferns.

What heights were reached by this genius in poetry, invention and imagination is shown by his greatest work, which was shown to me in his native town by the famous merchant DuFay in the year 1666, in which is depicted the *Contento*[1] or indulgence on a large copper panel in the following manner. In the air hovers Desire or Content depicted in two charming figures; below on earth several personages of high or low rank busy themselves, some worship the gods with devotion round a sacrificial fire, whilst in a dark temple the old priest, dressed in white, stands with the incense in the presence of Vestal Virgins crowned with laurel leaves, accompanied by youths in antique dress carrying vessels with caskets of incense and other implements for the altar, on which burns the sacrificial fire, by which the surrounding congregation are miraculously illuminated. In the front one sees the animals about to be slaughtered. From above the temple descends the terrible Jupiter with

1. Edinburgh, National Gallery

Overleaf: Il Contento, c. 1607.

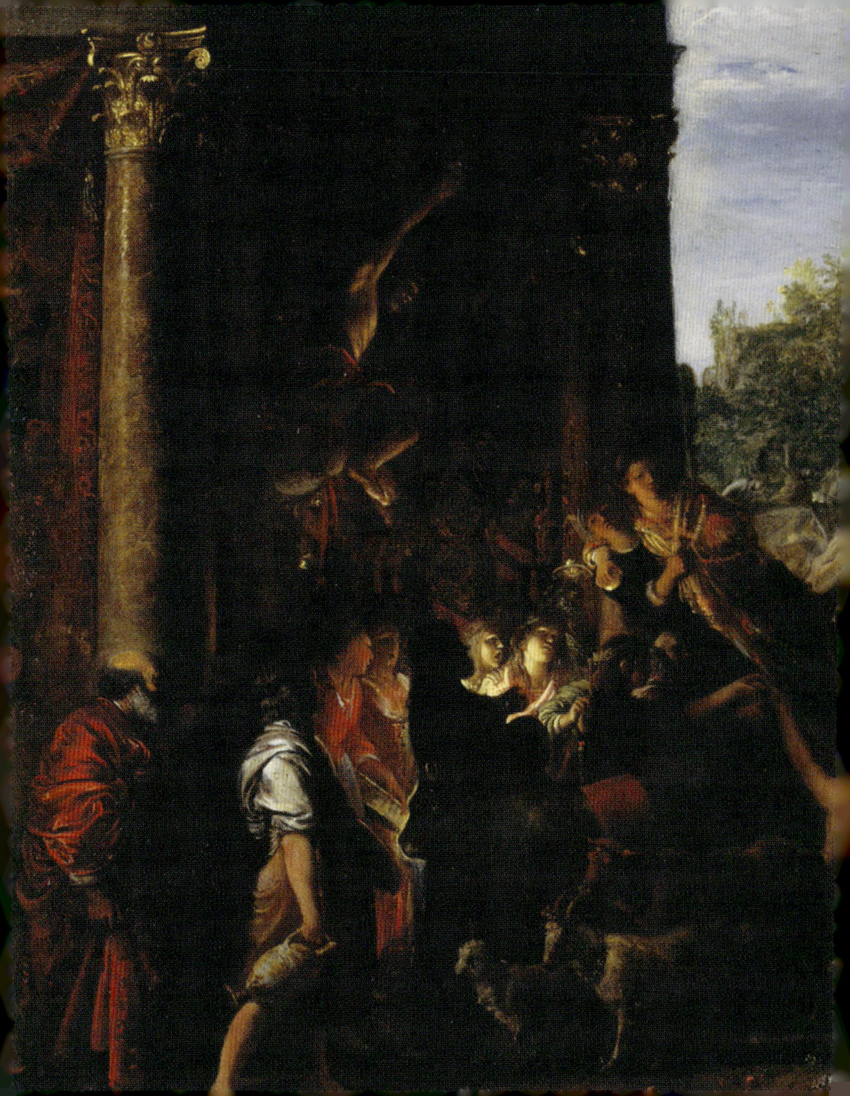

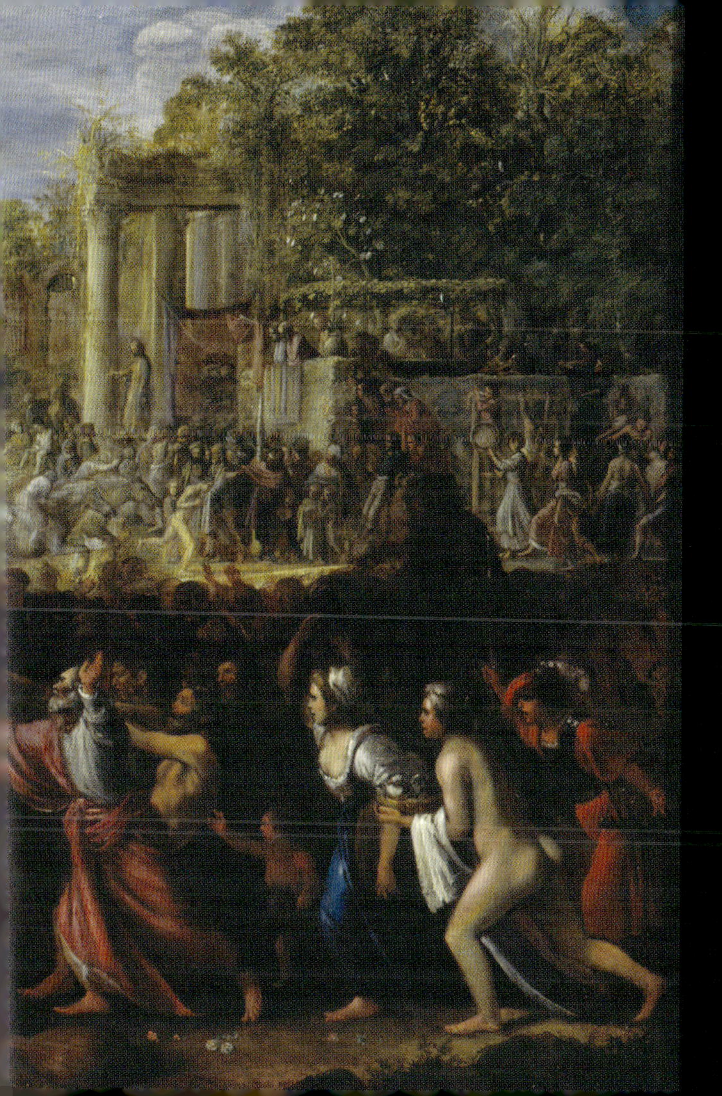

glittering thunderbolts in his hand, angrily noticing the sacrificial fire which has been lit for Contento. Outside the temple several personages are busy each according to his desires, eager for high position, splendour, wealth and possessions; the philosophers and others for scholarship, art and wisdom; others for gain through action and preparation for war; others again through sports such as running, horse-racing, bowling and gaming – all to gain content. All this has been rendered in such an original and curious manner that it must be for this town one of the greatest ornaments of the art of painting.

In another big piece he depicted the Flight into Egypt in which the Madonna sits on an ass and covers the child Jesus with her cloak.[1] Joseph, lighting the way with a burning torch in one hand, leads with the other the ass through a little brook bordered by plants. In the distance one sees herdsmen with their animals near a burning fire, which are reflected in the water. In the background a thick forest, above which are depicted in the clear sky the stars and especially the Milky Way and even more miraculously the clear full moon, which rises above the clouds on the

1. Munich, Alte Pinakothek, , illustrated p. 78

horizon, and whose reflection is perfectly rendered in the water, in a way which has never before been attempted. This work is incomparable both in the whole of its parts and in each individual part, as were all his works, of which he painted few, but excellently well on copper and which were used by Magdalena de Pas and others for engraving. The original, however, was often shown to me by Cavalier Goudt in Utrecht, a particular admirer of his art. And although he often attempted to engrave it on copper as faithfully as possible he was never able to reach complete excellence, because it is impossible that the art of engraving can equal that of painting. Although Goudt's engravings excel others, these engravings show up their inferiority when they are compared with the original paintings from which they were made – they are diminished in the same way as the earthly light is diminished and shamed by the clear sun.

So profound were Elsheimer's works, for his memory and imagination were thus constituted, that if he only saw a few beautiful trees (before which he had often sat or lain half or even whole days) they were

Overleaf: Flight into Egypt, 1609.

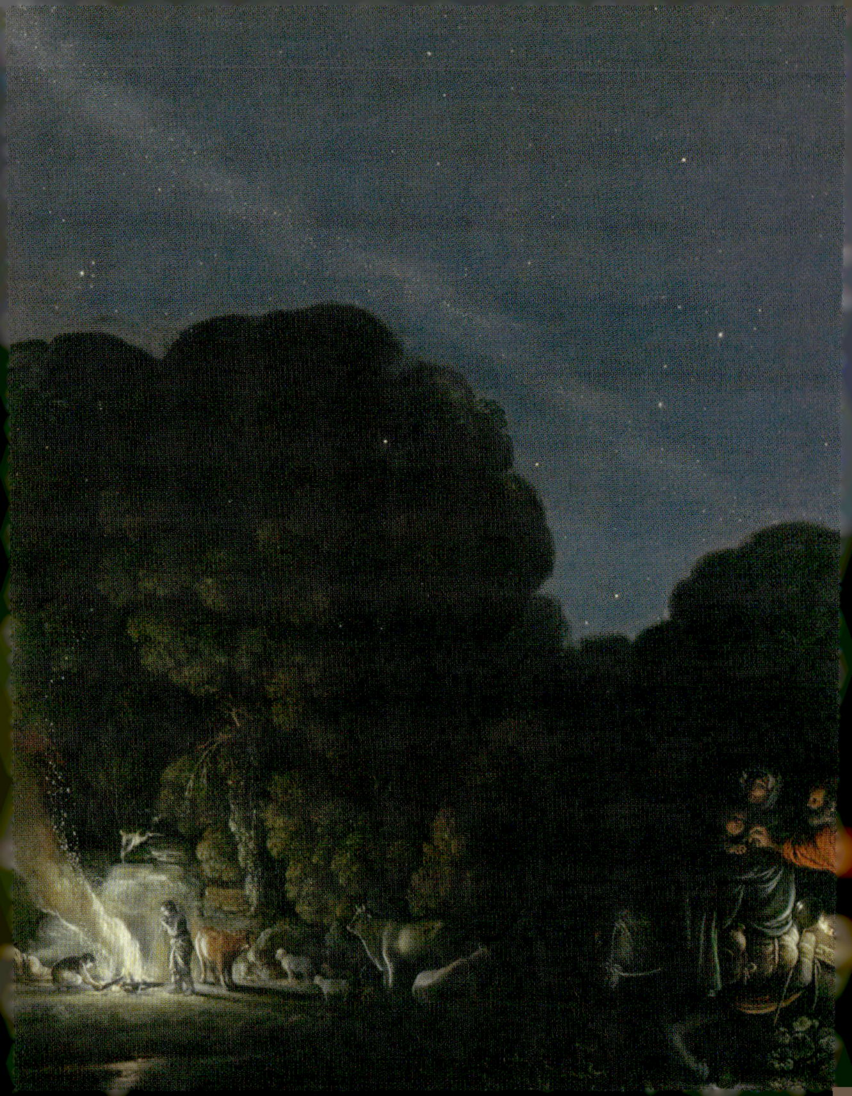

so firmly engraved on his mind that he was able to render a complete and natural likeness of them at home, without preliminary drawing. This can be judged by the fact that he impressed the Vigna Madama in Rome so firmly in his mind that he was able to incorporate it without any drawings and with greatest skill into his landscapes. Every tree is recognizable from its special type, from its stem, foliage and leaves in all parts as well as from colour, shade and reflection, quite similar, natural and vivid, a manner which not everybody can achieve and which is difficult without the aid of the actual object or a drawing. However, this difficult way of working made him finally tired and melancholic, as was his temperament in any case, and he neglected his domestic duties, for he married a Roman lady and had many children by her, hence he was poor although he received high payments for his works. Thus he became weary, ran into debts so that the above-mentioned Goudt had to encounter great expenses in Rome because he had advanced him money for work which was not being completed. As a result Elsheimer was put into the debtor's prison, where be did not even help himself by working (as he could and should well have done) but became so melancholic that he even became ill and although he was freed, he died soon afterwards in Rome, with immortal praise and echoes of his excellence. His widow, from whom I was able to acquire one of his works, still lived in Rome in 1632 with several surviving sons, whom my love of brevity prevents me from praising here any further. I only want to mention finally that Elsheimer not only invariably attempted difficult things, but he was also able to accomplish them splendidly. All his renderings surpassed by far the intentions of many other artists. His technique was so well grounded that even when he only drew an outline with pen or chalk, he showed more understanding than others were able even after steady painstaking effort. His works never consisted in fleeting movement, nor in mere decorative embellishment or loud colours, but above all and in every way in perfect draughtsmanship and natural colouring, so that if one compares his paintings with real life, as if in mirror-image, one would resemble the other. He had such a reputation in the wide, broad world, that all notable connoisseurs, as well as eager foreign travellers, expect to see something rare and important from his famous hand in the town hall of his native city, because he is universally called Adam of

Overleaf: Jupiter and Mercury with Philemon and Baucis, 1608-9.

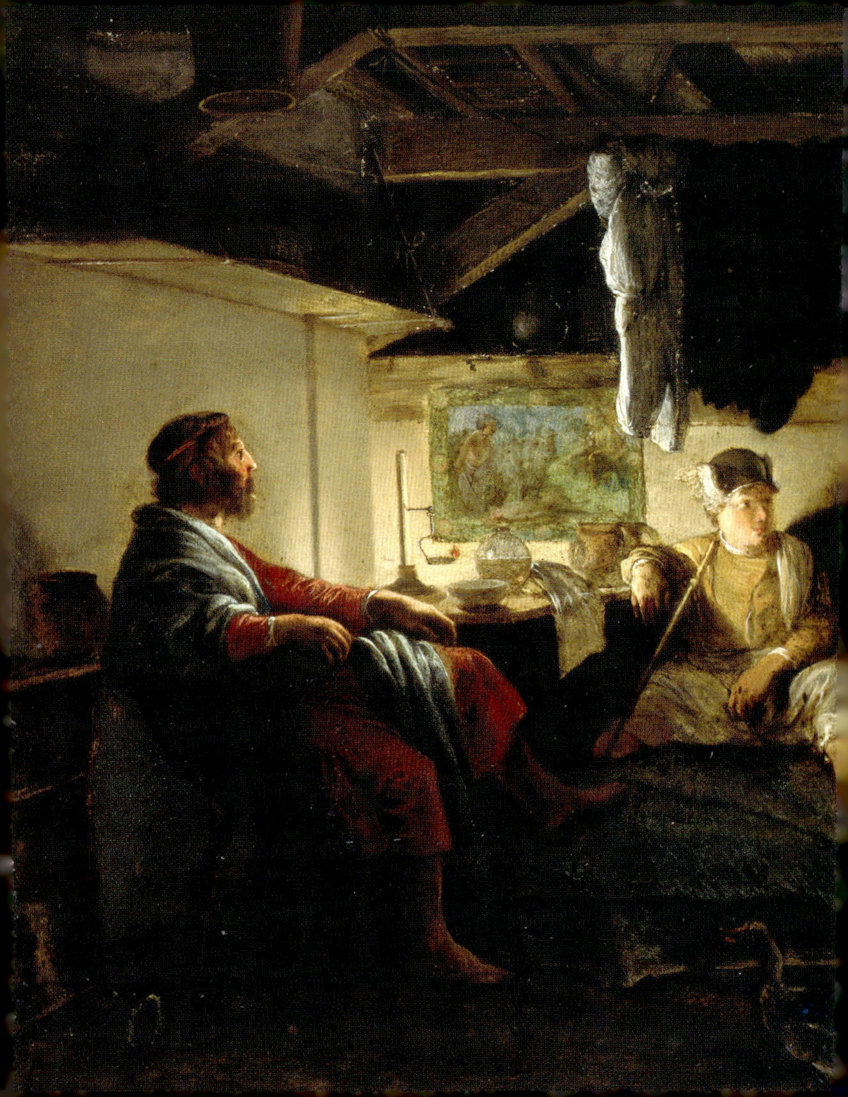

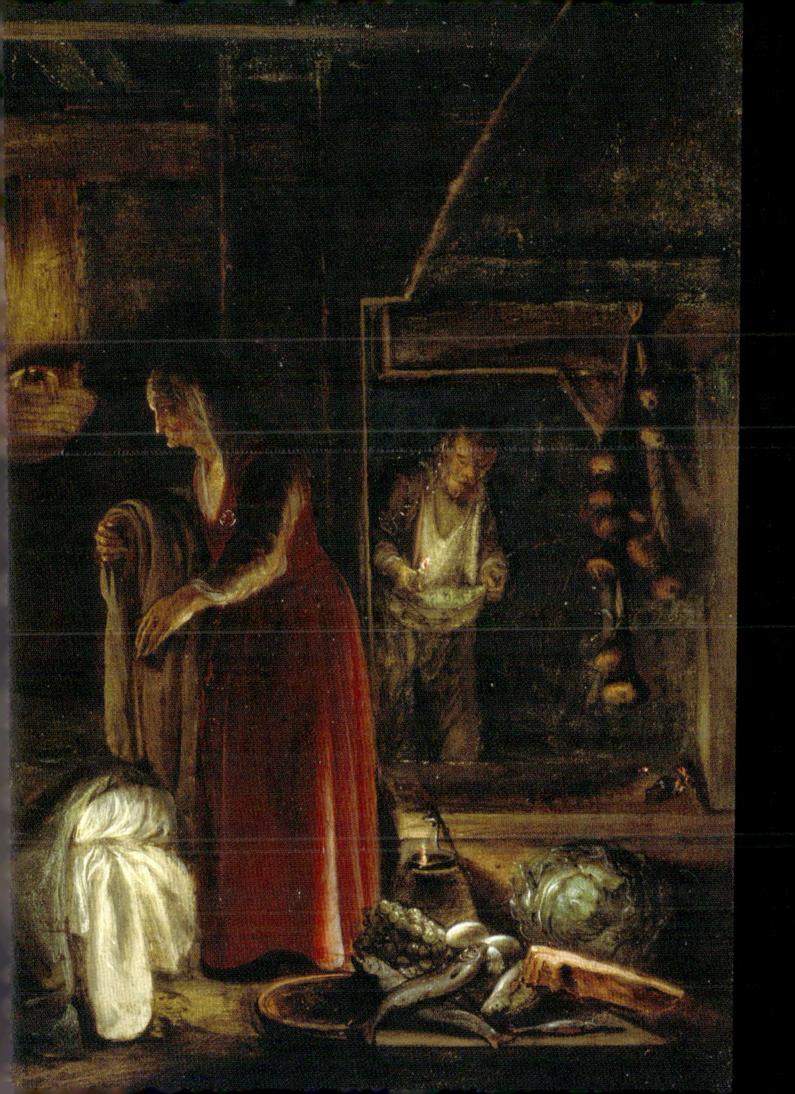

Frankfurt. And whilst Rome boasts with Raphael of Urbino, Florence with Michelangelo, Venice with Titian, Basle with Holbein, Nüremberg with Albrecht Dürer, Leiden with Lucas van Leiden, and other cities with other native works of art in their town halls to show to strangers and tourists as choice rarities, the noble magistrate of Frankfurt, which has a town hall filled with curiosities and works of art, cannot show a single work by this man, nor is his name commemorated, although there was in the past, and there is even now, the means and the opportunity to acquire some. In spite of this, however, the fame and glory of this praiseworthy artist will not fade, but it will be said of him:

As long as virtue will be loved
As long as the arts will flourish
So long one will be eager
To praise Elsheimer highly.

JEAN-BAPTISTE LE BRUN

The Life of Elsheimer

from

Galerie des Peintres

1792

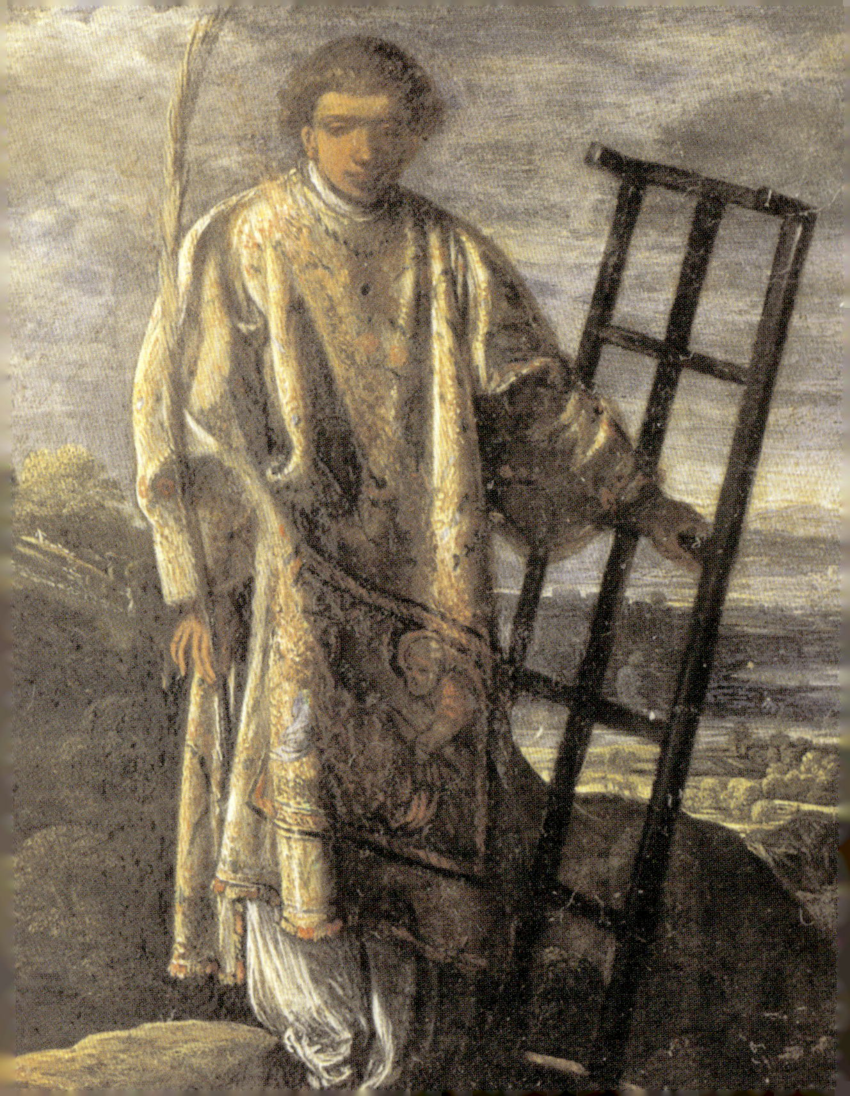

Adam Elsheimer was born at Frankfurt in 1574. His father, realizing his son's inclination for painting, placed him with Philipp Uffenbach, a good painter. Elsheimer left Germany to see Italy. It was there that he learned this manner of painting and finishing in a small format of which he made such a success. He was the best in the field in his time.

The paintings of this master are so many masterpieces; the delicacy of his brush is all the more astonishing for not preventing the achievement of rich colouring and a soft touch. His works are very rare today, and even so, one finds few which are well preserved, and therefore these fetch high prices; but one has to be on one's guard about a great number of copies made by Thoinan, Teniers the Elder, Bamboche [i.e. Pieter van Laer who left for Italy in 1623 and arrived in 1625] and Count Goudt. Many other painters also copied Elsheimer with success,

Opposite: St. Lawrence, c. 1605. This painting, from the same series as the Petworth paintings illustrated elsewhere, was once in the collection of the Grand Dukes of Tuscany, and was well known to French connoisseurs in the eighteenth century. It was acquired by the French Revolutionary-era painter François-Xavier Fabre during his long stay in Florence and is now in his eponymous museum in Montpellier

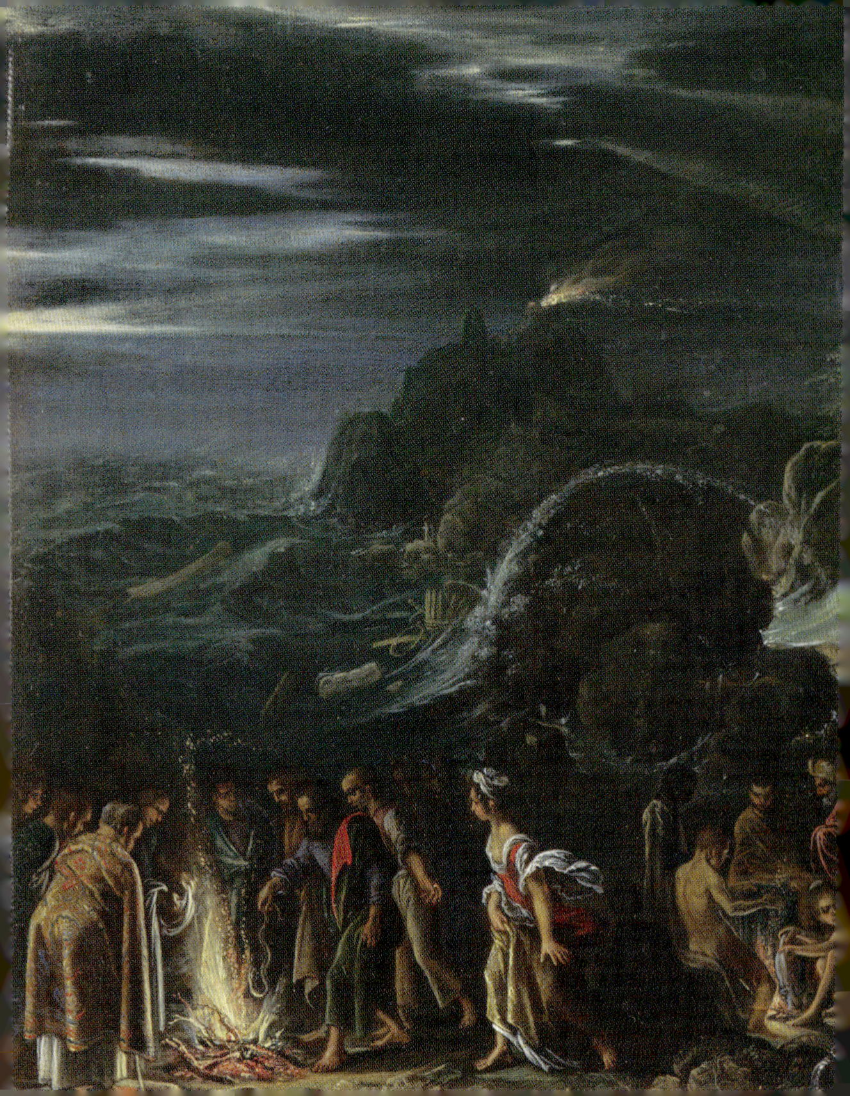

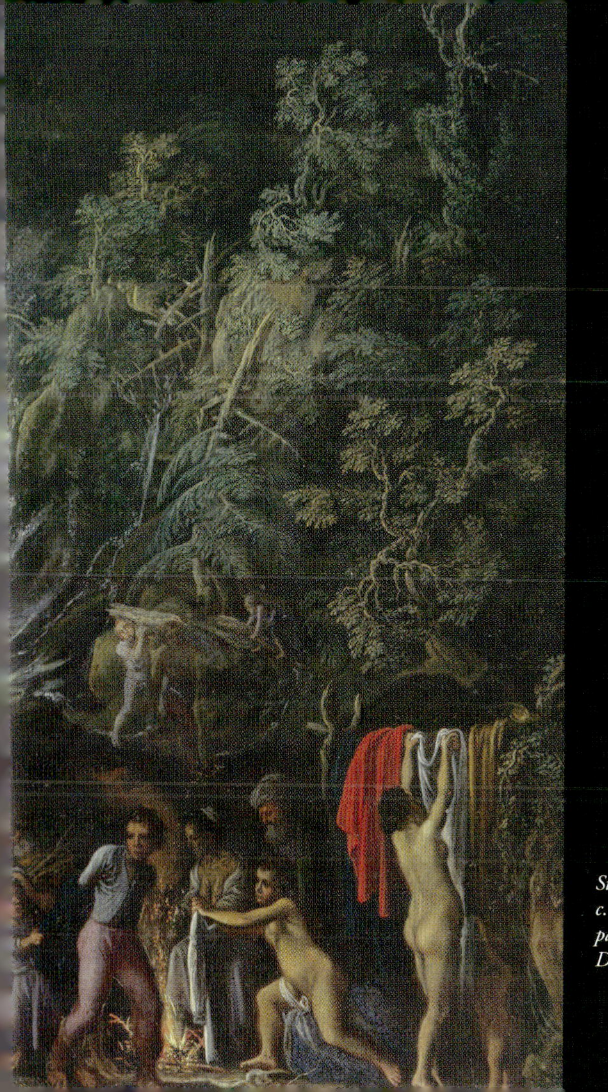

St Paul on Malta, c. 1600. One of the paintings copied by David Teniers

and when these paintings are from his time, it needs real connoisseurship and careful examination not to confuse them with the originals.

The little Moses, known under the name of Uytenbroeck, engraved several subjects of fables, landscapes and animals, being his own compositions in the manner of Elsheimer and Cornelis Poelenburgh.

Count Goudt, called Hendrik Goudt, has engraved seven paintings by Elsheimer, with great skill and effect. This painter has himself engraved several pieces of his own composition.

He died in Rome in 1620.

The price of the works of this master goes as high as 6000 livres and more, according to their richness and their composition. The one we had ourselves engraved [i.e. by Joseph Maillet] was sold for 1000 livres. His most excellent ones, although generally rare, are found in Germany. As he often used glazes a lot in painting, one finds them often over-cleaned through the ignorance of restorers.

PUPILS OF ELSHEIMER

Jakob Ernst Thoman von Hagelstein Hagelstein copied him and imitated his manner to the point of deception in his master's lifetime.

He was also copied by *[Jan Joost van] Cossiati*, painter to the Elector of Mainz at the castle of Schoenborn. This painter also painted several works in the 'ménagerie' at Versailles. He was born near Breda, and died in his seventies in Mainz in 1732 or 33.

Illustrations

Cover: Self-Portrait, Adam Elsheimer,
Uffizi, Florence
p. 1 Detail from The Baptism,
National Gallery, London
p. 2 The Stoning of St. Stephen, 34.7 x 28.6 cm,
National Gallery of Scotland, Edinburgh
p. 4 The Baptism, 28.1 x 21 cm,
National Gallery, London
p. 6 Judith and Holofernes, 23.2 x 17.8 cm,
The Wellington Museum, Apsley House, London
pp. 8-9 Conversion of Saul, 19.7 x 25.1 cm,
Städelsches Kunstinstitut und Städtische Gallerie,
Frankfurt am Main
pp. 12-13 The Flood, 26.5 x 34.8 cm,
Städelsches Kunstinstitut und Städtische Gallerie,
Frankfurt am Main
p. 15 The Three Maries at the Tomb, 25.8 x 20 cm
Rheinisches Landesmuseum, Bonn
pp. 18-19 The Realm of Venus, 8.7 x 14.6 cm,
Fitzwilliam Museum, Cambridge
pp. 22-23 The Realm of Minerva, 8.7 x 14.6 cm,
Fitzwilliam Museum, Cambridge
p. 25 St Paul, 9 x 7 cm,
Petworth House, The Egremont Collection (National Trust)
pp. 28-29 Aurora, 17 x 22.5 cm,
Herzog Anton Ulrich Museum, Braunschweig
pp. 28-29 Copy after Tobias and the Angel
('The Large Tobias'), 21 x 27 cm,
Statens Museum for Kunst, Copenhagen

p. 38 St John the Evangelist, 9 x 7 cm,
Petworth House, The Egremont Collection (National Trust)
p. 40 St John the Baptist, 9 x 7 cm,
Petworth House, The Egremont Collection (National Trust)
p. 42 St Elizabeth and the Virgin, 9 x 7 cm,
Petworth House, The Egremont Collection (National Trust)
p. 44 The Finding and the Exaltation of the True Cross,
'The Frankfurt Tabernacle', 125 x 100 cm overall
Städels und Städelscher Museums-Verein, Frankfurt am Main
p. 46 The Exaltation of the True Cross, 48.5 x 35 cm
Städels und Städelscher Museums-Verein, Frankfurt am Main
p. 48 The Embarkation of the Empress Helena, 22.5.5 x 14.9 cm
Städels und Städelscher Museums-Verein, Frankfurt am Main
p. 49 The Emperor Heraclius carrying the Cross
into Jerusalem, 22.5 x 15.3 cm,
Städels und Städelscher Museums-Verein, Frankfurt am Main
p. 52 Copy after The Mocking of Ceres, 29.5 x 24.1 cm,
Prado, Madrid
p. 56 Holy Family with the Infant St John, 37.5 x 24.3 cm,
Gemäldegalerie, Staatliche Museen, Berlin
p. 58-59 The Burning of Troy, 36 x 50 cm,
Alte Pinakothek, Bayerische Staatsgemäldesammlungen,
Munich
p. 61 The Witch, 13.5 x 9.8 cm, The Royal Collection,
© Her Majesty Queen Elizabeth II 2006
p. 64 The Beheading of John the Baptist, 7.8 x 6.7 cm,
Trustees of the Chatsworth Settlement, Chatsworth
pp. 65-66 Tobias and the Angel ('The Small Tobias'),
12.4 x 19.2 cm, Historisches Museum, Frankfurt
p. 69 Apollo and Coronis, 17.4 x 21.6 cm,
Walker Art Gallery, Liverpool

p. 70 St Lawrence being prepared for martyrdom,
26.7 x 20.6 cm, National Gallery, London
pp. 74-75 Il Contento, 30.1 x 42 cm,
National Gallery of Scotland, Edinburgh
pp. 78-79 The Flight into Egypt, 31 x 41 cm,
Alte Pinakothek, Bayerische Staatsgemäldesammlungen,
Munich
pp. 82-83 Jupiter and Mercury in the House of
Philemon and Baucis, 16.9 x 22.4 cm,
Gemäldegalerie, Staatliche Kunstsammlungen, Dresden
p. 86 St Lawrence, 9 x 7 cm,
Musée Fabre, Montpellier
pp. 88-89 Saint Paul on Malta, 17 x 21.3 cm,
National Gallery, London

Illustrations on pages
1, 8-9, 12-13, 15, 44, 46, 48, 49, 56, 58-59, 78-79, 82-83
courtesy of www.artothek.de

First published 2006 by Pallas Athene,
42 Spencer Rise, London NW5 1AP
www.pallasathene.co.uk

Printed in China

ISBN 1 86348 013 0
978 1 86348 013 0

Special thanks to
Claire Pace and Helen Langdon,

Textual Note:
The texts used in ths volume were all translated by
Keith Andrews
and grateful thanks are offered to his executor,
John Dick,
for permission to use them.